BEAGLING

BEAGLING

J.C. JEREMY HOBSON

Line drawings by Clare Pavey

David & Charles
Newton Abbot   London   North Pomfret (Vt)

To the Colne Valley Beagles, past members and present, but, most of all, to those of the late 1960s and early 1970s who were prepared to put up with a keen young lad, make him feel welcome and provide him with transport!

All black-and-white photographs are by Richard Hedger, unless otherwise indicated

British Library Cataloguing in Publication Data
Hobson, J.C. Jeremy
  Beagling.
  1. Beagling
  I. Title
  799.2'34   SF429.B3

  ISBN 0–7153–8923–8

Phototypeset by ABM Typographics Hull
and printed in Great Britain
by Redwood Burn Limited Trowbridge
for David & Charles Publishers plc
Brunel House Newton Abbot Devon

Published in the United States of America
by David & Charles Inc
North Pomfret Vermont 05053 USA

CONTENTS

1
WHY, WHAT AND WHERE

We'll all go a-hunting today,
All nature looks smiling and gay,
So we'll join the glad throng
    that goes laughing along.
And we'll all go a-hunting today.

'The Hunting Day'
W. WILLIAMS

Why follow the beagles?

To anyone who is keen, fit, energetic and fairly intelligent, there is
plenty of fun and exercise to be had from following hounds on foot
and never more than when the hounds are those which hunt the
hare.

Beagling could best be described as an intimate sport: the field is
tight and with the hounds for most of the day. It also has the advantage of not being fashionable or expensive and thus cluttered with
those people who appear purely to be seen wearing the right gear
and making the right noises and for no other reason. In this particular branch of venery there is no need to dress up and buy expensive
horses in order to follow hounds.

This is not meant to imply that foxhunting is in any way a lesser
sport than beagling. The foxhunters enjoy their day out every bit as
much as do those who follow the beagles but for very different
reasons.

Conditions which please the mounted foxhunter are, naturally, those least favourable to the follower on foot. Their reasons for following the beagles are an interest in houndwork and an enjoyment of a few precious hours spent in the open countryside when the rest of the week is spent indoors. Nor is beagling a sport restricted to participants of a certain age, whereas managing a horse capable of withstanding a hard day's foxhunting is, of necessity, a young and, possibly more importantly, a strong person's occupation.

There are also those amongst the foxhunting fraternity who hunt to ride and, provided that they get a good gallop, are probably not at all worried whether or not they see a hound for the whole of the day, and possibly only attend in order to qualify their horse for point-to-points or hunter trials. Others are there because it is the thing to do and in the hope that it may improve their social standing. A few may indeed be there because of a love of houndwork but it must be said that the latter group would probably do better to forgo their horses and instead take to Shanks's pony, which would give an increased chance of seeing hounds at close quarters, or, for the best of houndwork, they could come and watch the beagles!

Apart from the fact that there are few more enjoyable sights than a pack of beagles unvanned and that the late arrivals will miss this opening scenario, the newcomer will find it worth his while arriving at the scene of the meet at least a quarter of an hour before the advertised time in order to assess his fellow followers. If he tells the truth, that he is out to see some sport but hasn't the faintest idea of how to see it, where to go or what to look out for, there will be no shortage of advice.

Who goes beagling?

At least a couple of old country characters will be there and their trilby hats, long thick overcoats, plus fours and wellingtons will be recognised by anyone who has ever hunted with any pack, whether they be followers of foxhounds or harehounds. Although from first appearances it may seem a waste of time to approach them, the fact that they are never far away from their cars and yet still manage to see most of the action means that they can teach the tiro a lot about the likely movements of the hare, why a particular hound is good or bad and why the huntsman is doing as he is.

The follower will find that he has no need to be wary of these particular members of the field. They are so steeped in hunting know-

Young and old, there is no one type of person attracted to beagling

ledge that they will be only too pleased to talk to anyone of a like mind and, if your interest extends as far as a little bit of gossip and scandal then, with a nudge and a wink, they will probably be able to inform you of the affair between the huntsman and the female whipper-in! Indeed their lives are so involved with the hunt that it is not unknown for them to request that their ashes be spread somewhere on the hunt premises.

The landowner or farmer will also be there. After all, he must have an interest in the hounds, even if it is only a casual one, to have agreed to the meet taking place at all.

Arriving in the hound van will probably be a teenager of fifteen or sixteen and, unlikely as it may seem, this is probably one of the stalwarts of the hunt. In all likelihood he or she will have been at the kennels since early morning, swilling out, feeding the brood bitches and their puppies and preparing flesh to be fed to their pack upon their return.

Youthful enthusiasm knows no bounds and does not forget the hounds as soon as the hunting season finishes. These young people will continue to help out at the kennels throughout the summer and, as autumn approaches, they will have been entrusted to carry a whip during hound exercise. Eventually, as a reward for their endeavours, they will be carrying a whip on the hunting day and may also have been asked by the masters to wear full hunt uniform in order to act as fully fledged whippers-in.

Sometimes, when a hunt is affiliated to or is an integral part of a university, school or military establishment, a greater proportion of the field will consist of cadets and students. The beagles provide them with an important part of their recreational activities, although on occasions it might well be wondered by the casual observer whether certain individuals are not more interested in hunting for members of the opposite sex than they are in hunting the hare!

The masters and huntsmen of these packs are generally drawn from the students of the day and, in some instances, the welfare of the hounds and the management of the kennels is a job left entirely to the pupils, there being no permanent kennel staff employed.

Others may have the finances to keep a kennelman but even then the responsibility for the day-to-day chores such as skinning, draw-

Showing at the South of England Show. The Eton College on the flags in 1986

ing hounds for the hunting day, showing them at Peterborough or deciding from which bitch to breed will often fall to the students. Such involvement undoubtedly helps to create a greater understanding within the hunt but, because of the nature of education, college and military packs often face problems unknown by other hunts.

Without the continuity which a residential and permanent kennelman brings, there is no one to decide on a long-term breeding policy and when the masters are appointed annually they will all have their own ideas. Likewise, on the hunting day each master will have his own ideas on how to hunt hounds and in order that each might, literally and figuratively, have a fair crack of the whip, it is probably best if they agree amongst themselves that each should hunt the pack for a given period of time, say one term, rather than to try and alternate the hunting days, a process which will inevitably upset hounds. One master is bound to be a better, more natural huntsman than any of the others and hounds will obviously feel more at ease with him and so perform better in the field.

There could be further problems brought about by the long vacations. In instances where no permanent kennel staff is kept, there will often be no alternative but to arrange that certain parents who are fortunate enough to possess suitable kennels or outbuildings should take them on for the duration. By doing so I suppose that they are maintaining a tradition unique to the beagling world, as the majority of this type of pack originated from hounds which were in private ownership, and beagles which were brought to school by the sons of landed gentry in order to give them a little amusement during termtime were soon formed into a more permanent and well-organised unit with the establishment's name behind them.

College packs have gained themselves a reputation as being a good starting point for those who wish to enter into the foxhunting world and when one considers the fact that students also have a curriculum to abide by and exams to pass, it is no wonder that enthusiasm often becomes obsession and that those who are now merely masters of beagles will, in a few years' time, be very experienced and competent huntsmen and masters of foxhounds. Commander Forbes (Maintop), writing in *Hounds, Gentlemen, Please*, rues the fact that it is not within the range of practical politics to compel all foxhunters to begin their hunting career by a course of

'foot-beagling' and he quotes a passage from Mr Thomas Smith's
Life of a Fox:

> With foot-beagles all who go out seem to understand the game; even the
> beginners set to work to learn all about it; and very seldom do we see the
> field do anything to interfere in any way with the workings of the hounds.
> An ill advised holloa may sometimes be heard from an over excited indi-
> vidual, but, being sternly rebuked, he restrains his ardour and his lungs the
> next time. No one ever cackles when beagles come to a fault, because
> everyone wants to help the hounds, and knows that the best way to help
> them is to keep still and silent. Why should not foxhunters display the same
> interest in the hounds they follow?

The social side

Beagling is not all houndwork and hard work however. There is
also a very strong social side, and for some beagling is just an opportunity to mingle with friends of a like mind on a weekly basis.
They will always manage to find something new to talk about,
whether political or social, international or local. The meet often
provides a focal point for other interests: for instance the amateur
historian is bound to be interested in the fact that the green lane
over which he is walking was once a minor Roman road. And,
lastly, as well as giving him the opportunity to learn a lot more
about his immediate locality and countryside, following the
hounds often gives the beagler access to ground on which he would
otherwise be classed as a trespasser.

Raising the roof . . .

Depending on the venue, there may be a chance to indulge in some
socialising of a more liquid nature when the field returns to the meet
at the end of the day. Once 'beagling teas' were commonplace and,
after partaking of one of these gastronomic affairs, the beagler
would be replete almost until the next week when, hopefully, someone else would be kind enough to lay on another tea. Cambridge
University, at least, still struggles on manfully with this tradition
and when members of the Trinity Foot return the students possessing the largest rooms are often called upon to host one of these
gatherings.

In the absence of a beagling tea, most northern packs of beagles have the good sense to arrange their meets at a public house and, with the pubs opening at five o'clock (an hour earlier than those in the south), a good hunt which has continued until dark can be swiftly followed up with a pint and a discussion. If 'mine host' is genuinely interested in the beagles and makes the field really welcome, it is not unknown for the hounds to be taken back to the kennels and then for the hunt staff to return to the meet in order to join in the fun. When there are the makings of a good night, the pub staff will often provide trays of sandwiches even though they do not normally serve food. Before long, members and subscribers will be standing in order to sing their own particular hunting song with the rest of the room joining in with the chorus.

The hunting sing-song seems to be peculiar to the northern packs and nowhere are they more famous than in the Lake District, where the Fell packs' songs often represent hunts which actually took place. Persons named are often still living, or their families may still dwell in the same area. Songs are still regularly being written, proving that the happy tradition continues, and it is these which are adopted by the beagle packs who, fortified by some of the county's best bitter, will soon be raising the roof with 'Lil Melbreak', 'The Mardale Hunt', 'Dido, Bendigo', and, of course, 'John Peel', accompanied by holloas and horn-blowing which would indeed '. . . awaken the dead, or a fox from his lair in the morning'.

Whilst on the subject, it might be as well to mention for the benefit of those who attend such an evening for the first time that John Peel's coat was in fact grey, made from local skiddaw cloth, and not 'gay' as appears in most popular renditions of the song.

These impromptu gatherings do much to promote good relations amongst the followers and weld them into one happy family, with the hunt's best interests at heart.

. . . and money

Many hunts now boast a hunt supporters' club which followers can join and it is staggering just how successful such groups are at raising funds for the hunt. Many kennels would be without a decent hound van, cold store or new buildings, were it not for the efforts of these groups.

The schemes dreamt up by the supporters' committees are many and varied. Of course there are the usual events such as the cheese and wine party held at the kennels, which brings in money for very little outlay and effort, but what of the lengths some hunts go to in order to provide a day out not only for members and friends but also for the general public, some of whom may never have seen a beagle?

A country fair is quite an ambitious undertaking but, given a fair day weatherwise, the revenue which it brings it will go a long way towards financial security for the next twelve months. When the right atmosphere exists in the kennels and amongst supporters, it should be easy for the committee to delegate. The local farmer will provide the venue (free of charge, or course!) and any necessary straw bales, posts and rope. The neighbouring gamekeepers can run the gundog tests and either run a 'scurry' in which dogs are expected to retrieve dummies over obstacles and against the clock or invite contestants with spaniels and retrievers to undertake a course laid out on the lines of a working test. Another keeper, instead of watching his mate, can organise clay-pigeon shooting (which should be held well away from the main ring and anywhere else where the continuous banging may cause a distraction). There will be a parade of hounds kennelled in the locality, an easy thing to arrange by offering your hounds for other groups' events later in the year. And the committee member who for years has bored everyone to death with stories of how he and a certain famous celebrity are drinking partners can be called upon to prove his boast and get the celebrity to come and open the fair. All the usual attractions will thus soon be organised plus a few more which may be peculiar to the region. Local traders can be approached to rent a site on which to set up a stall and the hunt may be lucky enough to obtain sponsorship from some of these companies who will perhaps provide programmes free of charge in return for advertising.

An evening with a theme can often be quite successful. A 'Caribbean Evening' in which the village hall is transformed into a West Indian 'paradise' by the use of lobster pots, stuffed parrots, fishing nets and driftwood provides a novel experience and could well encourage a few extra people who would perhaps not be too bothered about turning out in order to attend the more normal type of evening's entertainment.

Most foxhound packs hold an annual point-to-point but it is unusual for a beagle pack to do the same. However, two exceptions to this rule are the Sandhurst and the Trinity Foot, the latter being run in conjunction with the Cambridgeshire Draghounds who share the same kennels. The true beagling equivalent of the point-to-point is the foot followers' steeplechase, a very strenuous affair which, as might be imagined, is a mixture of cross-country running and clambering (jumping would be too optimistic a word!) over various natural obstacles.

Probably the biggest and grandest event of the beagler's social calendar is the hunt ball which, with as many as five hundred people attending at twenty pounds or more a head, not surprisingly produces the greatest single sum raised in a year. Unfortunately not all of this is profit, as the ball is usually held in one of the area's better hotels and their bills are never cheap. The high price asked for a ticket never seems to deter subscribers and the secretary very often has to allocate tickets for the meal itself on a 'first come, first served' basis, producing a second, cheaper ticket for those who wish only to attend the dance. Hunt balls are occasionally held in London, there being no local hotels or venues large enough to accommodate all those who wish to attend. All of which goes to prove the continued and undoubted success of the oldest social function connected with any form of hunting.

As well as the events run purely and simply either to raise funds or to keep members in touch during the 'close' season, the hunt could do well to include some which are more in the way of a 'thank-you' to anyone who has helped during the season. The Aldershot Beagles, along with many others I am sure, hold a 'Keepers' Dinner' every March at which hunt staff, helpers, keepers, farmers and, most importantly, their wives or husbands, can sit down to a three-course meal for about £18 a double ticket, with drinks provided by the hunt. Whilst it might be thought that such an evening would turn into a cliquey affair with corners being taken up by keeper talking to keeper, farmer to farmer, in actual fact there will have been a good cross-section of discussion by the end of the evening.

An afternoon clay-pigeon shoot organised by the hunt for the same people is another possibility and when such a function is accompanied by a box or two of free cartridges and is then followed up with tea (both edible and drinkable) it has proved to be successful in helping to cement good relationships between the hunt and fellow country users.

Puppy shows

The puppy show is probably unique in being a combination of a way of saying 'thank you', a social event and, to a lesser extent, a fund-raiser. It will normally be held in May or June when the puppies which have been out to walk have had sufficient time to re-adjust to their life back in kennels. Once again the members of the hunt, keepers, members of adjacent hunts and all others who may be interested should be invited.

The judges, normally two in number and themselves masters of hounds, give prizes for the best dog, the best bitch and the best couple, with second and third prizes if the entry is large enough to justify it. The puppy walker whose hound is on the flags for the first time should remember that the judges will have their own particular preference for a certain type of hound but, win or lose, all the puppy walkers for the year will be given a small token, such as a silver spoon, in gratitude for their help and assistance.

When the pups have been duly displayed, admired and judged, there will be a few short speeches and then anyone who wishes can go through to the lodges and inspect the rest of the hounds before going to tea held in a suitable outbuilding or sometimes a marquee on the lawn. Afterwards there may be some form of evening entertainment, a barbecue perhaps or drinks at the huntsman's house, when, as the 'amber nectar' begins to flow, more speeches may be made. These can either be entertaining or very dull and fortunate indeed is the master who can not only keep his audience interested but is also able to achieve the right backing by choosing judges with the same happy knack.

No one should forget that the most important ingredients in the puppy show are the puppy walkers themselves and so they should be entertained in the best way possible in order to make them feel fully recompensed for all the trouble they have taken. If this is done properly, the puppy walkers will leave the kennels with the intention of taking one or two of next spring's puppies as soon as they become available.

Many of these walkers must go on for years and years without getting anywhere near the winning post but the experienced puppy walker will realise that, as the speaker at the annual school prize-giving is often fond of saying, 'It's not the winning that counts, but the taking part'. Nowhere is this more applicable than in the hunt kennels where the puppy walkers perform a very important task year after year.

At the puppy show the observer will notice that some of the young hounds have been given names which start with the same initials. This is no coincidence as it has long been the tradition of hunting packs to name all members of a litter with a form of identification which begins with the same letter. Such a procedure aids recognition by the hunt staff, especially when the names coincide with the same initial as was given to the dam. Rarely, if ever, however, is a litter given a name with the same initial as the stud dog. He is often from another kennel anyway and during the course of his life may sire many dozens of puppies in some of the ninety-odd beagle kennels scattered about the countryside.

Kennel visits

It is not necessary for the newcomer to beagling to wait until a function is being held before he makes a visit to the kennels in order to acquaint himself with both huntsman and hounds. Ideally, the kennels should be contacted in advance to make sure that a visit will be convenient but I have found that, without exception, popping in for a brief chat in order to introduce oneself will be turned into a comprehensive tour of the kennels with a cup of tea to follow. Nothing and no one seems to be too much trouble to the hunt staff once they realise that they are talking with someone who has as much interest in the sport as themselves.

There is always work to be done at the kennels, as we shall see when it comes to discussing life there in more detail, especially when one considers that most of the beagle packs are run by part-time amateurs and enthusiastic members of the field who give up a lot of their time to help with skinning, the collecting of flesh and general kennel maintenance. The visitor who has a certain professional skill such as building will be doubly welcome and encouraged to take a more active part in kennel life! But, for the rest and more seriously, it is stretching anyone's enthusiasm to turn up at a time when the kennels will be obviously busy. Early morning is clearly a bad time, when there is swilling out to be done and most kennels feed at that time anyway or at least prepare food for later in the day.

Those who know nothing about hounds will get a lot more

Skinning: one of the many daily jobs which must be carried out before hunt staff can be expected to entertain visitors

knowledge from a kennel visit if they tell the huntsman as much as soon as they arrive. One particular huntsman of my acquaintance will, as soon as anyone shows the first sign of interest in his hounds, tell the observer that 'they do look well, don't they? Understandably, after twenty-odd years in the same establishment and with the knowledge inherited from three generations of his family who were also involved with the care and hunting of beagles, he has every reason to be proud of his pack which shows incredible sport even on the most unlikely scenting days. But what good would he do showing these beagles to someone without much knowledge of the plus points? Few sights are more embarrassing than that of a huntsman drawing his best hounds one after another for the benefit of someone who has not the vaguest idea of what he is expected to say.

Even as the kennels themselves are bound to vary, so will any discipline shown during the visit. Whips should only be seen on the hunting field, for reasons described elsewhere. Provided that the hounds know the person who is mainly in charge, the raising of the voice should be enough to make them comply with the person's wishes. For one reason or another hounds may suddenly decide to 'pitch in' and in several of these cases a piece of alkathene tubing rattled against the railing seems to have the required effect, but arguably the most effective weapon in the disciplining of hounds is a bucket of water!

During a visit to the Aldershot beagles I was very impressed to see the splitting of dogs from bitches after the hunting day with a call of 'dog hounds, dog hounds'. After only a few seconds, the remainder left in the flesh house were bitches. Likewise, the dogs were fed first and when their allotted time was up they were sent quietly back to kennels, the carcass was turned over and the bitches were allowed in. At no time was there any disagreement amongst the pack and I was assured that the whole procedure was a result of early training with a bucket of water. So much better than whips and harsh words.

One reads accounts of kennels where no hound goes through any door without permission and the culmination of the 'show' occurs as hounds are brought out into a central yard, the main gates are thrown open, and the huntsman walks out and stands several yards away. Not until they receive the command from him are hounds allowed to move.

Those who have never seen it before will find interest in watching a pack of hounds being fed or in seeing them drawn by name for their meal, and to notice how the shy feeders and 'poor doers' are taken to one side and fed separately from the others. However, perhaps the most striking thing to stick in one's mind after a visit to the kennels will be, or indeed should be, the scrupulous cleanliness of every building, yard, corridor, sleeping house and, of course, feeding room, in many of which I would not have thought twice about eating my dinner from the floor.

There is a further point which may leave the visitor to the kennels a little confused and that occurs when a permanent kennel person is

Walter Clinkard after a successful showing season sometime in the 1930s. Son Roy is the third generation of a line which have devoted their lives to the welfare of beagling

employed. Very often one would be introduced to the kennel huntsman but, contrary to his title, he is not normally the person who hunts hounds and in beagle kennels especially he will, in all probability, be one of the whippers-in and responsible for the day-to-day running of the kennels. Foxhound packs call their member of staff 'kennelman' and, although he may be second in command, he would never venture out on to the hunting field. Nowadays, with money short and labour so expensive, there is inevitably consider-able interchange amongst any hunt staff's various duties and mas-ters often hunt their own hounds, quite frequently as amateurs, and so the kennelman is the only person professionally employed.

It may be wondered where the rest of the finances necessary for the successful running of a pack of beagles comes from and how it is administered. The events described earlier in this chapter – functions, open days, cheese and wine parties – all help towards the final goal, as do the all-important annual subscriptions.

The hunt committee

There is no difficulty in deciding on what to spend income but someone has to decide just what should be allocated where and attach differing degrees of importance to various projects. Obviously if the kennel roof has been blown off during the winter storms this will take precedence, but for the less alarming problems the financial dissection will fall upon members of the hunt committee.

Fortunately, it is no longer necessary for the master to have bottomless pockets in order to have the honour of adding the initials MH to his name although there is no doubt that being a master of hounds is still a fairly expensive and time-consuming affair. However, many of the decisions are now shared by his committee; in fact these are often now so influential that it is they who decide who is to become the next master.

There is a tremendous difference between a committee-run pack and a pack with a committee. In the latter case, the members are often merely figureheads, meeting only twice yearly with no one being really sure of their exact purpose. In fact, if someone is successful in losing the minutes of the previous meeting, and provided that there is an adequate supply of alcohol, so much the better!

When the pack is run by a committee which is responsible for the business side of hunting, however, things are very different.

The group is normally composed of a chairman, vice-chairman, secretary, treasurer and a number of enthusiastic members and followers, some of whom may be landowners or farmers.

Each hunt will have its own set of rules (most of which will be printed on the reverse side of the meet card) but in general it is the secretary and treasurer who are responsible for sending out cheques, dealing with all correspondence and reporting it to their fellow members as well as undertaking all the accounting which, like that of any other organisation, must be presented at the annual general meeting in the form of a balance sheet. After assessing just how much financial aid is likely to be required, the committee will then give a guarantee to provide a specific amount of money for the following year.

Things may differ slightly where a college or military pack is concerned and in certain circumstances the trustees of such establishments administer only the actual buildings, leaving the masters responsible for all other expenditure.

Further income may arise in the form of rent when, for instance, two or more packs of hounds share the same premises, but this is the exception rather than the rule. Two kennels where this does apply, however, are the Trinity Foot and the Sandhurst; both packs are able to allocate a certain proportion of the kennels to draghounds.

Sometimes the hunt will pay something towards its secretary's out-of-pocket expenses such as telephone calls, stamps and petrol but other than this he or she will give their services to the beagles free, content with the reward of a successful pack and a few outstanding hunting days.

Other members of the committee are every bit as important to the hunt as those with particular responsibilities. Where a kennel huntsman is not employed it is often these people who, once they have finished work for the day, will grab a quick meal at home and then rush off to the kennels in order to collect flesh, do an amount of skinning and wash down the yards. Their opinions should be respected at any meeting when they have something to say. It is all to easy for a committee to become divided between 'those who do' and 'those who merely talk about it'. The latter group often forms the majority, leaving three or four people to do the work and yet still managing to bulldoze items about which they know very little through the committee stages.

Hound identification

It will be a while before the newcomer to beagling is elected to any committee and, in the meantime, there is still much to be learnt. For instance at some time or another, whether it be on a hunting day or during the a visit to the kennels, as the follower bends down to fondle a particular hound he will perhaps notice that it has a tattoo on the inside of its ear. There are several points in favour of this system of identification, the first being that once a hound has been marked in this fashion there is no way that this can be destroyed; it is there for life. Given the fact that there are certain members of today's society who are interested in the beagle, whether it be to steal it in order to make money from offering such an animal for vivisection and research or, as happened to the Ecclesfield Beagles in 1985, as a protest against hunting by a group of 'antis', there will be no doubt as to a tattooed hound's ownership should it be recovered.

The Association of Masters of Harriers and Beagles rules that all hounds which are registered with it must be earmarked with the initials of the pack and also the litter number or letter, and that these marks must be made known to the association in order to avoid any possible confusion. There will obviously be several packs around the country whose names begin with the same letter but there are ways and means of overcoming this. The Catterick, Cheshire, Chilmark and Claro all start with the same initial and for them all to add a 'B' for beagle would result in just as much confusion as if they were not to bother. On a 'first come, first served' basis, the Chilmark are known simply by a 'C', the Cheshire with 'CB' and, for the rest, the next letter in the name is included so that, respectively, they become 'CA' and 'CL'.

Ear tattoos: an undisputable means of identifying members of a particular pack

The hunting year

Another point of general interest to the tiro is the fact that, rather like the Chinese who, with their year of the cat, dog, rat *et al*, celebrate their New Year at a different time to the majority of the western world, people employed or involved in the countryside have their own start to the year.

The farmer's calendar is full of sacred dates on which events are supposed to take place. For example, the weather on Candlemas Day, 2 February, was likely to indicate the weather for the following growing season but Lady Day, 25 March (incidentally the date on which it has long been thought that fox cubs are born), when rents were paid and labourers were 'hired and fired', was the start of the farmer's year. The gamekeeper's year traditionally starts on the first of February, the water bailiff's on the first of October. As far as the hunting world is concerned, the first of May is the all-important date.

Although nowadays it is mainly an academic starter to the year, nevertheless any staff which are employed will probably take office from this date. When a committee is responsible for appointing a new master or joint masters, an advertisement will be placed in the national press to coincide with this date, telling would-be candidates what will be expected of them in terms of the number of days' hunting and how much money is available.

Helpful advice

There is also the matter of etiquette and the newcomer to beagling should be aware of some of the more useful courtesies both on and off the hunting field.

When one knows the master personally, it would of course be rather pretentious to make a big deal of saying, 'Good morning, master,' during an informal visit to the kennels but at the meet he should be acknowledged in just this fashion and if you happen to be near him (or her, for there are many female masters) at the end of day, 'good night' and a comment on a good day's hunting should be the form. If, on the other hand, the day has left a lot to be desired, there is no need to make any adverse remarks; after all the master, of all people, will already know this fact. Above all else, never criticise the hunting while in the field: it is one of the worst breaches of hunting manners, for which no excuse is good enough. Although after a little experience has been gained one is certain that the huntsman has made the wrong cast, or that a particular hound has been seen on numerous occasions to be skirting or babbling, these comments should be left unsaid. There will be plenty of time to mention these facts diplomatically either at the kennels or during the post-hunting singsong at the local and, who knows, once the crisis has passed your ideas may even be appreciated! Likewise, if one should inadvertently get into trouble with the hunt staff, do not answer back or argue; again there will be a far better opportunity to explain one's actions later in the day.

In an effort to avoid any trouble, keep downwind of the pack and never walk in front of the hounds: by doing so, one runs the risk of foiling the scent and spoiling not only your sport but that of many others.

Unless there is a specific reason for doing so, the hunt staff should not be distracted whilst hunting is taking place. A lot can happen if for instance a whipper-in turns to chat about the weather or accept a cigarette from a follower and a split-second delay in his actions as a result could prove to be potentially dangerous if he is positioned to stop hounds running towards a busy road or railway line.

There are a few further oddments of general advice which may be of interest to the beagler before he attends his first day's hunting and which, one day, he may thank me for mentioning!

Although the question of footwear is dealt with fully in a later chapter, always take with you a change of stockings and shoes. It is almost certain that your feet will get wet and muddy, which is both dangerous and uncomfortable when it comes to the end of the day and it is time to drive home.

A certain amount of loose change should always be carried, even at the risk of losing it as one jumps over one obstacle or another. Accidents will happen and it may be necessary to use a telephone. The beagler may have become so enthused with his day's sport that he finds he has overestimated his walking capacity and, in the absence of any fellow followers travelling by car, may need to get a bus back to the meet or home. Even if he is able to thumb a lift, some reward will be very acceptable to the kind-hearted driver. Perhaps most importantly, some money will be required for the 'cap'.

In country which contains much wire, it may unfortunately be

Taking the 'cap'. Frank Martin, secretary to the Aldershot beagles, capping Mrs Martin

the lot of the follower to witness a hound becoming hung up in the top strand. This is especially likely when the fence is made up of sheep netting topped off by a couple of strands of barbed wire. Before rushing in to help, it is as well to bear in mind that not only will you be a stranger to the animal but it will also be badly frightened. When taking hold, therefore, take a firm grip and keep it if you want to avoid being bitten. If the hound is obviously going to bite and it is impossible to muzzle it in some way, a piece of stick is the best equivalent of the cowboy's bullet for it to chew on.

It may be that the area over which you are hunting is keepered and that the keeper needs to set fox wires in order to protect his pheasants. Although a good keeper will make every effort to pick up his snares before the arrival of the beagles, one of them may be forgotten and a hound wandering off on its own may become caught. Throw a coat over its head before attempting to release it and do not expect it to appear grateful for being released: in all probability it will merely run off in an effort to catch up with the rest of the pack. Some masters and huntsmen get a bit funny about members of the field dragging the odd lost hound about on the end of a piece of string in an effort to return it to the 'fold'. Break the rule about distracting the whipper-in if there is one close and ask his opinion on how best to deal with the matter.

Planning the meet card

As this chapter is entitled 'Why, What and Where', the newcomer to the sport may well wonder why a particular venue is decided upon and what the criteria are for a good meeting point.

Answered simply, the venue should provide plenty of hares with the potential for showing good sport and the best meeting point is one which supporters and subscribers will find easily. If not a pub car park or village green, it is likely to be a local landmark. For example, the Aldershot Beagles meet at 'the grain dryer' a couple of times a season and, apart from being told the name of the nearest village, that is the only information volunteered. Not much to go on, one might think, but, with the knowledge of a grid reference and if one drives long enough, a fine set of grain dryers will be seen as one turns a corner. Before long, then, the keen follower will discover places he never knew existed and the venues will hold no mystery.

Many of the meets are traditional and are handed down from one set of masters to the next. The most obvious of these is the Boxing Day meet which, irrespective of whether the pack contains foxhounds, harriers or beagles, will be held in the same place year after year. Local events are often commemorated with a meet of hounds and the Colne Valley and Holme Valley disregard their normal hunting days of Saturdays, Tuesdays and Wednesdays to combine and hold a meet on a Monday at Jackson Bridge in order to retain the memory of a past huntsman. This annual event is known as the Barrow hunt.

Normally, however, the meet cards are the responsibility of the masters and it is up to them to ensure that all parts of the area are evenly hunted. If one venue were favoured because of its density of hares and was consequently overhunted, then it would not be long before the pack began to experience a few blank days, not because they had killed off all the hares (the season's total of kills for most packs is very small considering the number of days hunted) but more likely because of excessive disturbance.

Certain meets do undoubtedly contain hares which are easier to catch than they would be in another locality, the reason for which is not really known but could be due to the topography. A. G. Allen Turner, contributing a piece on beagling to the second volume of *The House of Sport* published in 1899, gave this explanation:

> Leicestershire hares, too, are generally real strong ones, and the explanation of this, given me some years ago by another master, may account for the fact. His words were – "Hares here are always in hard condition because they get coursed day after day by sheepdogs as the shepherds go their rounds."
>
> In heavier countries, with much plough and little grass, one wants bigger and stronger hounds, or they will have little or no chance of killing hares. Thirteen-inch hounds [what pack today contains 13 inch hounds?!] will kill a hare, even in such countries, with a blazing scent and luck, but they will not stand the hard work for long, and, as a rule, will soon be run out of scent by a good hare.

Local farmers may like to see hounds and be prepared to put on a lawn meet or tea, irrespective of whether or not the ground is full of hares, and their wishes must be catered for. After all, beaglers are dependent on landowners for their sport and it must be remembered that the man who owns 25 acres of ground is just as important as the one who is able to boast 2,500. The hunt crosses both their estates only as guests and is just as likely to cause damage or annoyance to the one as it is to the other.

Although beagling is not likely to cause as much disturbance to the shooting estate as is foxhunting, a list of shooting days from local estates will undoubtedly help when planning the meet card.

There has always been a certain amount of friction between hunting and shooting and it was in an effort to dispel some of the myths that the *Shooting Times* put so much effort into research on how foxhunting can in fact tie in with shooting. Their displays at many game fairs during the late 1970s proved it was possible to draw coverts for a fox on the Wednesday and still have an excellent day's shooting on the Saturday. The problem in the past has been that there was no 'give and take'. For instance, Egerton Warburton wrote:

> Since one fox more diversion will bring
> Than twice twenty thousand cock pheasants on wing,

The author feeding his young poults . . .
. . . and beagling

Why, What and Where

That man we all honour, whate'er be his rank,
Whose heart heaves a sigh when his gorse is drawn blank.

Gamekeepers can without fail give examples of how hounds have
ruined their sport, a point which will be extended in the final chapter, but some shoots feel that hounds can only do good by stirring
up the pheasants and preparing them to fly well for the first day's
shooting.

Being employed as a gamekeeper and being obsessed by beagling,
I have been torn between two camps. Never has the expression
'hunting with the hare and running with the hounds' been more appropriate. On one estate where I worked, if we had a fox which was
proving difficult to catch the first inclination was to telephone the
local pack of beagles. Usually on a Sunday morning they would
bring three couple of hounds and would draw through a few likely
places. The keepers would have gathered half a dozen good shots
and be standing at the end of the wood and in this way a whole litter
of well-grown cubs would often be accounted for.

The hare is almost always found on open farmland and there is
no real reason for the beagles to enter a wood full of pheasants but
the fact remains that, in the early part of the season at least, many of
the year's poults will be gleaning the stubble and travelling the
hedgerows and it is this fact which must be borne in mind when
planning the meets. Although it can be very annoying for a master
of hounds and his committee to get requests that this particular part
of the farm must not be disturbed by hounds, they should remember that it is much more annoying to shooters who have probably paid a lot of money and have been anticipating a favourite
stand for weeks, if not months, to arrive at the pheasant or par-
tridge cover only to see hounds running through it. This is probably
the greatest cause of friction between the hunting man and the
shooting tenant but it is without doubt extremely difficult for the
huntsman to stop his hounds on a well-run hare which they obviously deserve to kill. Remember the man with 25 acres, for although his shooting probably only concerns himself, a friend, a dog
and a dozen pheasants reared under a broody bantam, he will be
looking forward to his Saturday afternoon's sport with just as
much excitement as the business magnate to his day of five or six
hundred birds in the bag.

When arranging new meets, the master who lives in the locality

The rough shooter has as much right to expect consideration from the hunt as has the landowner with thousands of acres

starts off with a great advantage as he is probably going to meet the majority of landowners at business lunches or at some of the various dinner parties to which he is asked.

In cases where there are several joint masters it may be as well to split the country into areas and let each master be responsible for a particular area, drawing up a list of those landlords to be contacted before the start of the season. In the event that one of the masters is responsible both for hunting and for the general well-being of the hounds in kennels, the other 'joints' should leave him with his charges. He will undoubtedly already be doing more than his fair share of liaising with farmers and the like as hound exercise and flesh collection will keep him in close contact with these people throughout the year.

Another point to bear in mind when planning the meet card is that of the various farming practices carried out in a particular area. It is no use approaching a sheep farmer for one of the meets at the end of the season when it is obvious that he will have fields full of in-lamb ewes or indeed, now that the fashion seems to be for earlier and earlier lambings, ewes which have already lambed.

But, whatever the situation in a certain country, it is unlikely that the masters and huntsmen of any hounds will be able to fix their meets in the same casual manner that the Brookside Harriers who hunted the area around Lewes in Sussex fixed theirs in the early part of this century. Their meet card looked like this:

Brookside Harriers (Lewes)
Appointments for the season.

Mondays at Newmarket Hill.
Thursdays at Telscombe Tye.

On the back of the card was printed a line map of the country, showing the location of the two meets. What would today's masters give for a location which allowed such arrangements? Obviously each meet offered a choice of hunting in at least four different directions but how many hares must the area have contained in order to supply excellent hunting year after year?

To quote again from A. G. Allen Turner on beagling in *The House of Sport:*

Tis the middle of November, and a still day, with just that crispness in the air which makes one feel a man, as we draw nine couple of sixteen-inch hounds from the kennels, and start on our seven miles tramp to the meet, which is in the best part of our country, with hares just plentiful enough for sport, and the farmers always glad to see us. Punctually at eleven o'clock, we arrive, and are joined by about a dozen members of the hunt, three or four ladies, and half a dozen farmers. Five minutes chat, and a refresher for some of us, and then we move off down the road, into a meadow. At the far side of this is a cluster of holly bushes, which has, for years, been a sure

The Meon Valley beagles with joint-master and huntsman, Mr Charles Vivian, moving off from a lawn meet at Droxford, Hampshire *(Geoff Burch)*

find. She is not at home to-day, however, and we cross another meadow to a big field, stretching down towards the railway. We make a line across this, and draw downhill (the kennelmen having been previously sent ahead to stop hounds at the line if a train is signalled) . . . One whip runs forward on either side of the covert as they reach it . . . A keeper now comes up and asks us not to disturb the covert further, as it is to be shot again in a week's time, so we have reluctantly to whip off, leaving, no doubt, a fairly beaten hare behind . . . We are three miles away from where we found . . . As it will soon be dark, and we have a seven mile tramp back to kennels, we knock off at four thirty.

A hard day, for men, and hounds, and after a well earned drink with one of our good friends, the farmers, we light our pipes, and home is the word. We shall be tired when we get there . . . and after a hot bath and a light dinner (a heavy one is a great mistake after a hard day's beagling), we shall have our smoke and turn in early.

These few words, written almost a century ago, describe not only the why but also the what and where, for beagling's continued popularity in the late 1980s.

The Meon Valley beagles drawing for their hare *(Geoff Burch)*

2
THE HUNTING DAY

Probably the greatest advantage beagling has over its fellow country sports is that an active involvement does not leave a hole in the pocket. There is no horse and stable to keep up, no expensive guns and cartridges to buy, no need to wince every spring when the invitation to renew one's membership of the fly-fishers' club comes through the letterbox, necessitating of course the purchase of the latest carbon-fibre rod and its attendant accessories, but, perhaps best of all, there is no need for any special clothing which, for all the other activities, seems so expensive and so essential.

What to wear

The newcomer to the sport may wonder what to wear for his first appearance in the hunting field but his eventual apparel will often depend upon how active he intends to be. Following the pack alone and without the experience of other members of the hunt, the newcomer may be tempted to stick closely to the huntsman and chase after hounds, once they have found. After pursuing them up hill and down dale, he may decide to run after hounds dressed only in pumps, shorts and sweater, but he should remember that not all the day is spent running after beagles and quite a lot of it is spent standing around watching hounds at a check or drawing for a fresh hare. The top of a hill in January in a cold north wind is not the most comfortable of places, and windproof clothing is an advantage.

Most country-orientated people possess a waxed waterproof

coat of the type which Barbour sell and this could provide a good basis for the beagler's wardrobe. A pair of 'plus twos', loose enough to allow negotiation of the tightest barbed-wire fence, preferably made from a thornproof or fine whipcord material, coupled with a pair of thick woollen stockings, which are traditionally knitted in beagling green, provide the ideal clothing for the nether regions and, in exceptionally severe weather, a pair of 'long johns' will help to prevent any chapping from the cold wind.

With the addition of a woollen jumper or waistcoat and a flannel shirt, all that remains is the question of footwear. This item applies to the whole field, or at any rate to those who intend to run rather than stand about. Probably the most effective is a canvas shoe with a crepe sole, which has the great advantage of lightness. The modern trainer or hockey boot also helps to support the foot and ankle, a fact which is so necessary when beagling on stony ground. The followers of a pack of hounds which hunts continually on hard, flinty ground, such as in the North or on the downlands, may well decide to eschew the regulation hockey boot in favour of the more traditional leather variety.

The hunt staff needs to be in contact with their hounds at all times and because of this, no matter what the topography and terrain, they will in all probability be wearing canvas boots of the type previously mentioned. They know that they will be lucky to get through the day without wet feet and so the ability to travel across a ploughed field quickly without picking up enough clay to make a dinner service becomes the most important factor. The casual follower, on the other hand, may get away with wellington boots — at least until he decides whether or not beagling is the sport for him — but if he intends to follow the hounds on a permanent basis they should soon be replaced. Basically, 'hunt in comfort' should apply to the field and the follower should leave it to the hunt officials to dress the part.

Most of the clothing which the hunt staff wears has a practical value, with the possible exception of the heavy hunting hat which most masters expect their employees to wear and which is often worn purely and simply for the sake of tradition. This can be got round, if rather expensively, by buying a velvet-covered cork hat which weighs as little as 1 ounce but probably the most practical headgear is a green flat cap as this has the advantage of lightness and yet still conforms to the master's ideas of smartness. After all, the hat is not intended to save the hunter's skull, as in the case of the foxhunter.

The stock is not decorative: on a wet day it will prevent water from running down the wearer's neck and, in the rare event of a serious accident, it can be used as an emergency bandage. The hunt coat, normally green for hare-hunting packs, serves not only to protect the wearer from the cold and wet but also identifies him as a member of the hunt to the followers and subscribers. Green is the traditional colour but several beagle packs have broken with this tradition for one reason or another. The Warwickshire, for instance, clothe their hunt staff in plum-coloured jackets, simply because their founder, Guy Jackson, donned his father's smoking jacket on a hunting day! The Britannia, being a naval pack hunting in the Dartmouth area, wear a coat of navy blue, the Eton College one of brown, whilst the Holme Valley in common with the Derbyshire, Nottinghamshire and Staffordshire Beagles equip their huntsmen with a coat of hunting 'pink'. In the latter instance the tradition started when the originator of the pack, George Manners, decided that he preferred the colour. Packs like the Old Berkeley show their affiliation with their big brothers of the foxhunting world by attaching a collar of Berkeley yellow to the usual green hare-hunter's coat, the Old Berkeley Foxhounds being most unusual in putting their hunt servants in coats of mustard yellow.

Breeches are always white, again a very practical colour for enabling the follower to distinguish members of the hunt staff, although the people responsible for cleaning the breeches would probably not agree when they are called upon to wash the clothes of a whipper-in who has travelled across many muddy fields during the course of the day and then returned to the kennels in the back of the hound van! The white does undoubtedly help the follower to understand what is going on as it stands out against the background of a wood or spinney.

Apart from the horn carried in a specially designed pocket by the huntsman, probably the most important item of equipment carried by the hunt staff is the whip. Although it is not used to hit hounds physically, a crack accompanied with some harsh words from the whippers-in is often the only means of getting rioting beagles off the scent of deer, for instance. Again, on occasions serious injuries as hounds head towards a busy road or railway will only be prevented by some prompt action with whip and voice.

The Hunting Day

Like the colour of their jackets, the whips carried by foxhunters differ from those carried by beaglers. The foxhunter's crop is equipped with an L-shaped, horn handle which is useful for gaining extra inches on the arms when attempting to shut gates from horseback. The beagler's whip is usually capped by a rather smart silver ball, decorative but absolutely useless when it comes to hauling oneself from the bottom of a ditch surrounding the Lincolnshire fens, and for this reason alone members of the hunt staff will often do better to purchase a whip of the kind used by the foxhunting fraternity.

Unless asked by the committee and masters, the casual follower cannot just decide to appear with a whip but perhaps a stick will provide him with a means of remaining upright when the going gets rough. A small pair of binoculars which can be kept in the pocket when running after hounds may also prove useful.

How to get there

Putting aside the question of clothes for the moment, the potential beagler now has to make contact with his local pack in order to find out on what days hunting is carried out, the likely venues and the times of the meets. With the advent of anti-bloodsport groups, the days have long gone when every pub pinned up a fixture list of meets in the bar for all to see, or the local paper published the meets for the following week for both the foxhunting and the beagling packs, and the newcomer is probably best advised to seek out someone who is known by the hunt. Once he is known to be genuinely interested, members of the hunt will undoubtedly bend over backwards in order to make the new beagler well and truly welcome: cups of tea, transport to the meets in the hound van and lessons in recognising the pack's individual hound members will soon be offered.

It is usual for most packs nowadays to hunt once a day, twice weekly, normally starting at 12.30 or 1.30pm. There are obviously variations to this, however; the school and college packs, for instance, often cannot commence their hunting until 2pm as students carry out the kennelwork themselves and this in turn has to fit in with the curriculum. One or two packs, especially in the north, do manage two hunts in the same day and have separate meets at around 10.30am and at 2pm (originally planned so as to allow mill

Unvanning the pack: Michael Jackson preparing the Sandhurst beagles for a day's hunting

workers some sport in between shift work). Where the hare popula-tion allows it, both meets may be from the same venue, but for others it is necessary to van on to another part of the country for the afternoon meet.

The most common starting point is likely to be a public house but the meet can be held virtually anywhere — a farmyard, beauty spot car park, village green, or merely at the side of the road close to a local landmark. Lawn meets and hospitality are sometimes offered by a member of the hunt who is fortunate to have enough room to allow for parking and enough sherry glasses to hold the 'stirrup cup' but in fact the host can be anyone in the country with an interest in the hunt. Although a follower may live in country which is hunted by another pack, it may still be possible for him to hold a lawn meet and then hounds could either be taken back into their own country or, provided that the master has first obtained permis-sion from the master or committee of that country (including any foxhound packs) and the words 'By invitation' have been written on the advertised meet card, the guest pack could hunt from there. This is often an ideal way to let beaglers from other areas see how hounds cope with ground which is sometimes different in terrain from the type which they normally hunt.

Now that transporting hounds is no problem, many packs take them literally to the other end of the country for a few days' hunting. This tradition was probably started by the Trinity Foot Beagles who, many years ago, began taking their hounds to Northumberland and created what has become known as the Northumberland Beagling Festival, a very popular event which takes place every September with several packs travelling up for the week and each being given a day on which to hunt. Other packs have their own favourite 'holiday' spots — the Colne Valley, for instance, visiting the Lake District and hunting ground normally covered by the Melbreak Foxhounds. Incidentally, this visit is timed to coincide with the Melbreak's Hunt Ball, which is itself an event not to be missed!

Once at the meet and unvanned, the pack is usually kept together in a tight bunch around the master and huntsman for a few minutes in order to give the supporters a chance to see hounds before they move off to the first draw.

Hounds at the meet

It will be noticed that a mixed pack of dogs and bitches is generally used and only a few of today's 'crack' foxhound packs hunt a dog and bitch pack on separate days. Most masters and huntsmen feel that it is a mistake to use only doghounds because by themselves they tend to be a little too headstrong. The inclusion of bitches has a calming influence, making for a more even pack. A small pack which is hunted on a shoestring may decide to keep only bitches in their kennels, borrowing a stallion hound from another hunt when they feel a need to breed another litter of puppies, but such a hunt is probably a rarity. The majority of packs keep an average of twenty to thirty couple of hounds in kennels.

How many hounds are brought to the meet depends on several things. Before deciding which hounds to bring, the master, huntsman or kennelman will probably have walked out with the pack or at least let them into the grass run in order to look them over and check them for fitness. To keep a certain standard of fitness amongst the hounds, it is logical to take as many to the meet as is possible. Regular hunting has the advantage of making hounds steadier but they cannot normally be expected to hunt on more than five days per fortnight.

A meet held mid-week could run into problems if too large a pack is taken to an area which is heavily wooded or with a high population of deer. If, due to the pressures of work, only one or two whippers-in are likely to be present, the huntsman is asking for trouble taking out too many hounds in the fond belief that he can control them: they will undoubtedly riot on deer.

As hounds mingle round the huntsman at the meet, it is an interesting exercise for the observer to try and count the numbers of hounds out on that particular day, remembering that they are always counted in couples, one beagle forming half a couple. Although archaic and somewhat reminiscent of the old-time shepherd counting his flock in what seems to the listener to be another language, in practice this method of counting hounds is much easier than trying to add up the numbers individually and it will be noticed that where an opportunity arises, say for instance as hounds go through a gate or scramble between a fence or stile, one or another of the whippers-in will count them and report to the huntsman that they are 'all on'. Regular checks of this nature will help to identify a certain point where a member of the pack has separated from its fellows and, at the end of the day, will provide a good starting point from which to look for it. For one reason or another, hounds do become separated from the rest of the pack and where this is seen the animal should be encouraged by the followers to return to the job in hand. A hound light at the end of the day is not normally a cause for too great a concern as beagles are very intelligent animals and will either return to the kennels, if they are close enough, or to the meet, where the farmer or publican can usually catch them and telephone the kennels.

The size and colouring of the hounds will also be of interest to the onlooker. Whilst 'a good horse is never a bad colour', it will be noticed that there is an obvious preference for a certain type, whether it be lemon and white or of the more traditional foxhound colour of black, tan and white. Those with plenty of white about them will be much the easiest to see when in chase but the colouring will have arisen because of the preferences of master or huntsman and hopefully in achieving a colour to their liking they have not foregone the more important points of nose and hunting ability.

Counting hounds back into the van at the end of the day. Through the day the whips will have been counting hounds at every available opportunity. A hound light at the end of the day is not normally, however, a cause for great concern; it will be picked up by hunt staff later that evening or the following morning *(Geoff Burch)*

The size of the hounds will depend upon the type of country to be hunted. The difference in height between one pack and another is not, as was overheard on the hunting field recently, because the hunt with the bigger hounds is using older and more mature ones and the pack with the smaller type are taking out younger hounds which are not yet fully grown! An average size and height is around 15 inches but hounds which hunt over moorland and stone walls will probably be a little taller than this and, conversely, hounds which hunt over flat grassland or arable and have never seen a ditch, wall or fence, other than perhaps a barbed-wire one, will be quite a bit smaller. Most masters like to show their hounds at some of the larger agricultural shows which combine hound classes (notably the Great Yorkshire, South of England, Honiton and the Royal Welsh) or at one of the specialised events such as Peterborough or Rydal, and to do so their hounds must not exceed 16 inches in height. At 17 inches a hound becomes a harrier, which in turn must not be more than 21 inches at the shoulder. If the newcomer is hunting with a pack calling themselves 'hare hounds', he is likely to notice a very mixed pack which could contain a few beagles drafted from a hunt because of their large size, several bassets and perhaps a small proportion of harriers.

Some huntsmen consider speed is important and therefore breed a hound which is small, light-boned and 'racy', feeling that more ground will be covered and that hounds will still be capable of sorting themselves out at a check. However there can be no point in having hounds that are too fast as they cannot cover the ground any faster than their nose will pick up the scent. When a country contains many hares, such breeding has proved fatal.

Whatever the size, a level pack is important and although the well-matched hounds look pretty standing around the legs of the huntsman it is not merely for cosmetic reasons that they are chosen. Beagles which are almost uniformly well matched and carefully selected in respect to speed will hunt together as a pack rather than as individuals, and the beagler will not have been hunting long before he hears it said that the pack hunted so well and so close together that 'a tablecloth could have been dropped over them and covered them all'. Actually, when the saying originated, probably from the book *Sportsman's Cabinet* published in 1804, it was said that hounds could be covered by a 'sheet', which is slightly larger than a tablecloth; but still, no matter, possibly a pack contained more couples of hounds in those days!

Moving off and hunting happenings

To return to the meet, the plans for the day will have been thoroughly discussed by the hunt staff on their way to the meet and, once the huntsman has blown a few sharp notes to signal that he is moving off, the follower will notice that at least two or three of the whippers-in will leave the rest of the group in order to place themselves ready for any potential action. Their exact whereabouts will depend on the country about to be hunted. If the area is heavily

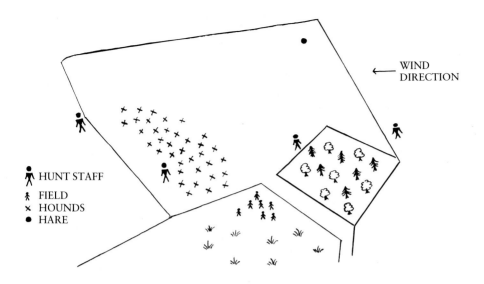

WIND
DIRECTION

HUNT STAFF
FIELD
HOUNDS
HARE

Positioning hounds and staff for the draw

With a wind direction from east to west as shown, the huntsman would probably take hounds in on the bottom left-hand side of the field so as to make the best use of the available scenting conditions. The watching field should be kept back so as not to foil any scent. The huntsman is, naturally, at the centre of the pack, whilst the three whippers-in are positioned so as to be able to cope with any problem which may arise. Once the hare has been found, she will probably run away from hounds and field. The two whips on the left and right will be able to run forward and watch the direction of the hunted hare. The third whip has been instructed to remain with his back to the wood, and will be expected to stay there for the duration of the hunt, as the land-owner has pheasants in the vicinity and is anxious that this particular covert is not disturbed

wooded and the meet is taking place during the shooting season, the estate gamekeeper will not be too pleased if hounds hunt right through his best covers, disturbing birds which are best left quiet for the shoot on Saturday. Roe deer, too, could prove something of a problem if the 'whips' are not positioned in such a way as to be able to stop hounds if they show any inclination to riot.

The remainder of the whippers-in will probably flank the huntsman until he arrives at the first field to be drawn, when they will then spread out, the better to assist him.

In most cases, the huntsman will check on the wind direction be-fore deciding which way to draw. By working his hounds upwind so that, should there be a hare in the area, her scent will be carried towards them, he is giving his pack the best possible chance.

Throughout the draw, it will be noticed that the huntsman is

As hounds move off to the first draw, the whippers-in normally flank the pack before spreading out in order to assist the huntsman

using his voice in order to encourage his hounds, for one of the greatest mistakes he can make is to draw for a hare by using his horn instead of his voice. The horn should never be used unless he wants his hounds to move towards him. Unlike foxhunting, the first part of the draw will be seen by the majority of the field and there is no need for the huntsman to use his horn to let them know what is happening. Too frequent a use of the horn will have the effect of either making hounds move towards him, thus defeating all attempts which may have been made to achieve a wide-ranging pack, or else the hounds will pay increasingly little attention because of the horn's incessant noise.

The horn plays an important part in the day's hunting and the would-be beagler should try to identify what the various calls mean, the better to understand what is happening. If one is fortunate enough to be following a well-disciplined pack with a good reputation, it will not be long before the follower can make an intelligent guess as to what is going on by watching the reaction of the hounds on hearing the horn and by observing the movements of the 'whips', who will often be able to receive their instructions in this way. As a very general rule, short, sharp notes are used to encourage hounds or to call them back to whoever is hunting them, whilst the long, mournful notes denote the end of the day or a kill.

As the hounds spread out in their search for a hare, the huntsman should regulate his pace to that of his hounds. He will find that they will, of their own accord, draw through a short cropped field as fast as he can walk, whereas when the cover is thicker, say in rough ground full of reeds, they will slow down and draw more carefully.

Some years ago it was usual for the beagle packs to appoint a field master who was responsible for the direct control of the field. At the draw he would line up the followers behind hounds and persuade them to advance in formation so as to be able to put up any hares which the hounds may have missed. To me, this seems a rather unsporting thing to do; after all, if the pack is any good, they should be able to find a hare without any help of this nature. Nowadays, one of the joint masters or perhaps the hunt treasurer or secretary is usually left to keep an eye on the field and discipline seems to be a little less strict, with members being allowed to wander where they will, providing of course that they do not get in front of hounds or otherwise disrupt the proceedings.

It might be as well to mention at this point, whilst talking of the treasurer and secretary, that one or the other of them will probably

'Owning' the scent: hounds begin to feather before dashing off

After casting, one or two of the older more experienced hounds pick up the scent again and begin to give tongue . . .

. . . very soon the remainder of the pack joins in

48

be wearing an armband with the initials CAP embroidered on it, and it is to him that the casual follower should pay a small amount of money for the privilege of hunting with the pack. There is usually no need to look for him: the 'cap' man will try and get around the field at the meet, but if hounds move off before he has seen every one you can rest assured that he will remember who has 'capped' and who has not and you will be approached before the afternoon's sport has finished. Most hunts have a set rate which they expect any follower who does not pay an annual subscription to donate, but it is not likely to 'break the bank' and it is unusual for the going rate to be more than a couple of pounds, thus proving the statement made at the outset of this chapter as to how inexpensive the sport of beagling really is. What other activity, even including your petrol, can be followed so cheaply? Even the annual subscription paid by regular members of the hunt is unlikely to exceed the £75 mark. No wonder, then, that there are so many people watching the huntsman making his first draw.

As he does so, one or two of the older hounds may begin to feather, indicating that the field contains some kind of scent. For a

Roy Clinkard about to step in and help his pack pick up the scent after they have made every effort to help themselves. Notice how some hounds are already looking towards their huntsman for assistance *(Geoff Burch)*

moment or two, the huntsman should stand still and keep quiet as the rest of the pack try to own the scene. On a good scenting day, and if a hare has recently left the area, the whole group of hounds will begin to give tongue. It is only then that the huntsman should give a cheer or two and perhaps 'double' his horn in order to encourage his hounds and let the late arrivals know what is happening.

When hounds get away on the scent, there will be a certain amount of excitement amongst members of the field as the more energetic of them run on in pursuit of the huntsman. The more experienced will probably head towards the nearest vantage point, a position from which they will be reluctant to move and from where they will see most of the action.

As a general rule, it will not be long before the first check is encountered and in their excitement, particularly if this is the first hare of the day, hounds will probably overrun the scent. It is then imperative that they should be allowed to make their own cast before the huntsman decides to give them a hand.

A good, knowledgeable field will have kept back a little way behind the pack and as soon as they notice that the pack has lost the scent they will stop and remain quiet. If they can be made to realise that most of the hunt can be seen from quite some way off, and to act accordingly, the whole proceedings will be greatly improved and so will the huntsman's chances of giving them a good day. Instead of the crowds pressing on his hounds, they will have all the space they want to cast in any direction. Experts reckon that if they are allowed to do this at the first check they will hunt better for the rest of the day, and so there should be no sound of chattering and laughter which will undoubtedly distract hounds and tempt them to lift their heads.

With no distractions, the hounds should be given every chance to pick up the scent for themselves and should not be helped until they have actually given up trying and are standing around with their heads up looking at their huntsman, who should then walk quietly into the middle of them and make his cast.

When casting, the hounds should be positioned either in front of

---

(*above*) Aldershot 'Welcome' 86, with some of the rosettes won by the pack in recent years (*Richard Hedger*)
(*below*) A bitch from the Aldershot beagles with her litter of day-old pups (*Richard Hedger*)

the huntsman or well to one flank; they should not be trailing along behind him and those hounds which do so could well find themselves listed for drafting at the end of the season. By watching his pack, the huntsman will be able to notice any indications which they may give him as to the way they think the hare has gone and, because he is behind or to one side of hounds, there is no danger of him fouling the ground in front of them.

Where should he make his cast? Well, the answer to this will depend on a number of points. He will have noticed the exact spot where hounds first lost the scent, bearing in mind that some of the faster hounds may well have overshot the mark by several yards. If, as a good huntsman, he knows the capacities of each individual hound, he will ignore these and watch the older, more experienced ones hesitating where the scent finally failed. The field will probably be able to help. It is unlikely that the hare will have run towards a group of them without being spotted but even in their excitement they should resist the temptation to holloa in order to attract the huntsman's attention; instead they should make known a view by holding up their cap, handkerchief or merely a hand. The huntsman can then choose whether or not to use the information and lift the beagles to the view or let them continue working it out for themselves. There is always the danger that a hare viewed by one of the field at some distance from the hounds is not necessarily the hunted one, although she might at first appear to be a run hare. In an area where many hares are to be found, it is possible that hounds may have a brace travelling in front of them. However, if the follower is absolutely certain that it *is* the hunted hare which he has seen and the huntsman cannot see a hat or hand held up in the air, then as a last resort a holloa is permissible; but it should be remembered that one should never shout unless one is close to the ground over which the hare has passed. It will cause the greatest annoyance to the huntsman when he runs to a holloa with his pack to be told by the shouter that the hare has gone away over the hill in the vicinity where hounds checked and his own cast would have hit off the line in less time than it took him to get to the holloa.

Two of the entry *(Richard Hedger)*
The young entry at the Aldershot beagles' annual puppy show *(Richard Hedger)*

Generally, when a hare is first roused, she is not unduly worried. The ears are upright and she merely 'slopes' away . . .

As hounds press, however, her ears will probably be laid down flat; legs outstretched and body at full length. The hunted hare's body seems closer to the ground than usual and her coat will become darker, either from sweat or mud

Should the huntsman find that he arrives with little more than half his pack with him, he must make the best of a bad job and go on with whatever hounds he has, blowing the horn until the majority are up with him.

Unless systematically performed, the process of laying hounds on to the line can be a disastrous one, for if the huntsman is not careful when hounds eventually do touch the scent again, they may set off on a heel trail. To be on the safe side, therefore, the huntsman should position himself on the side of the pack from which the hare is known to have come so that he can stop them at once should they start hunting in the wrong direction. Drawing hounds diagonally across the line can also help to prevent this but if it is done at too acute an angle he may not hit off the line at all, for the information given by the person who holloaed may not be accurate to within 10 yards or so, or else the scent may have been carried downwind.

Very occasionally, with accurate information given to the huntsman and prompt attention from hounds, it is possible for the beagler to watch a spectacular piece of hunting as the huntsman takes off his hat and sweeps both his hat and his arm over the line, hounds running straight to his signal, picking up the scent and running on, all in one glorious movement, giving the impression from a distance that his beagles are about to disappear up the huntsman's sleeve. On a weak or catchy scent, however, it is probably of no use whatsoever to lift hounds to a holloa but it is on those days when scent is neither good nor bad that help may be useful to the pack, though even then they should be allowed to try and recover the line themselves if at all possible. Given such a chance, and provided that they have plenty of room, the older members of the pack will soon pick up the scent and their chorus will bring the rest back. It is far better to let them do this cast for themselves; if they are successful in picking up the scent unaided, they will hunt a lot steadier for the rest of the day.

Whilst drawing and casting, it is not uncommon for hounds to be led off by a rabbit or sometimes a gamebird, especially when (as often happens) the pack checks where the hare has pushed through the hedge and in order to own the line again they have to hunt up and down the bottom of the hedgerow. It is the duty of the nearest hunt official to restore order on such occasions by voice and whip. Even the most disciplined of packs are not entirely free of lapses into riot; after all, although exasperating to the huntsman, it is really hard to blame a hound mistaking a rabbit for the hare for which he is searching.

The huntsman has a duty to try and show good sport to the followers. In the absence of a view and with no obvious scent to speak of, he cannot leave matters too long before deciding where to make his cast, that is, deciding where the scent petered out or where the hare was last seen, and a more vigorous effort must be made if he is

Calling hounds back after rioting on a rabbit

to show the field that he knows his job. He must not disappoint his hounds either and no doubt, in the time that he has spent watching them trying to pick up the scent on their own, he will have a few ideas of his own on how to help them. By this time it will probably have become evident that the hare is running either right or left handed and a cast may be tried on the appropriate side. (An allowance must be made for a crosswind, as the scent may be picked up by hounds many yards away from where the hare actually travelled.) If this fails, the huntsman will probably take the hounds forward a few yards and begin drawing in a small circle which is then enlarged to cover the point just short of the actual place where the hounds lost their hare. By doing so he is likely to lead the hounds across her line. As a hare will almost always be back on her home ground within two hours of being found, possibly the next cast will be made over the shortest way back to where she was first found and hounds put across the way she would probably take to reach it.

There is always the chance that the hare may not have gone anywhere at all and could be still squatting close to where she was lost, in which case, should hounds put her up again after a good run and a prolonged draw, a disappointing hunt may ensue before she is killed very quickly, stiffness and cramp making her an easy victim. Several years ago an old and knowledgeable countryman, experienced in all forms of fieldsports, told me that he did not agree with beagling for this very reason. Even when a hunted hare has got away and been given best, he felt that she should probably die during the cold night after such strenuous exertion.

Some huntsmen feel that to kill a hare in such disppointing circumstances, or even occasionally to chop one before she has had a chance to run, is preferable to going out for several hunting days without killing, with the risk of hounds losing interest and some of their hunting ability. There can be no doubt that after an unsuccessful day hounds do go back to kennels feeling frustrated (in human terms, that is) and fights in the van during the journey home or in the lodges are more likely to break out than if the day was terminated by a kill. Others are convinced that beagles run more for the love of following the scent than for the joy of tasting the actual fruits of their labours. C. B. Shepherd, one-time master of the South Hertfordshire Beagles, wrote in 1938:

> I have seen hounds hunting downhill overtake the hare, kill her and leave her, and race straight on after what, I presume, must have been the scent blown forward by the breeze. On one occasion hounds killed a hare and a second hare got up within a few yards. They immediately left the kill and went off after the second hare and eventually caught her also, when exactly the same happened again. At the end of the third run, we had three hares to break up together. This appears to me to prove that the fascination of actual hunting has far more attraction to the hound than the break up of the hare once it has ceased to run. On one occasion when hounds were casting for a very tired hare, a freshly entered pup came upon her, and, instead of making any effort at dispatching her, he pushed her along with his muzzle to make her run again. He evidently thought it quite unreasonable of the hare to stop his fun, merely to have a rest.

Whatever the details, there are few masters and huntsmen who do not agree that it is essential for a pack to be 'in blood' but, as we have seen, it is on the subject of 'being in blood' that they differ. Many will say that hounds are out of blood if they go out three days running without killing a hare; others, for instance, say that the magic period is three weeks. So much depends on hunt staff, hounds and the country that surely there can be no hard and fast rules?

When a hare is killed, if the pads and mask are required as mementos of a particularly good hunt the corpse should be retrieved as quickly as possible and then thrown back to the hounds for them to break up. This should be done whilst they are still excited and if, when they are doing so, the huntsman blows the horn notes which he normally uses when the hare has gone away, he will teach hounds that there is something exciting going on and that they had better stick with him unless they want to miss the fun. Although to the onlooker such apparent enjoyment of the kill may seem a little macabre and ghoulish, especially when the hunt members present scream and shout as if it is the best thing they have ever seen in their lives, such encouragement is absolutely necessary especially if there are young, recently entered puppies out with the pack. Later on, the huntsman can revert to whatever notes he normally reserves for the kill in order to inform members of the field who did not see what happened.

The Association of Masters of Harriers and Beagles sets out a strict code of conduct concerning the sport of hare hunting and insists, upon threat of expulsion, that no pack of hounds of which the master is a member of the asasociation shall be allowed to hunt a hare which has previously been in any form of captivity or in any way handled or is otherwise not in 'her wild and natural state'. These rules are even more important as hounds begin to catch up with their tiring hare. Should a hare be run to ground (and it is surprising just how many times a hare will disappear down a drain, for instance) there are two alternatives which the huntsman can take. The first and most obvious is to leave her where she is. Second, if for one reason or another it is considered advisable to kill her, she must be extracted and immediately destroyed before being given to the hounds to break up, thus abiding by the ethics of good sportsmanship and being as humane as possible.

No hare which is carrying young should knowingly be hunted and for this reason every effort must be made not to fix any meets after the end of March at the latest.

The association quite rightly and sensibly suggests that every effort must be made to prevent hounds hunting a hare through the gardens of a town or village, and should the hare then enter a house or building they must be taken away and the hare left. The master should then inform the owner or occupier in order to ascertain how he or she would like the hare to be dealt with. Obviously it is better if these circumstances do not arise and the less opportunity the general public and the media have for casting aspersions on the sport, the better.

The behaviour of not only the hunt staff but also members of the field is very important, especially when there are many followers out for the afternoon bringing with them more chance of potential damage. One person can scramble over a gate or stone wall without leaving any trace but the same cannot be said if perhaps as many as a hundred pairs of feet tread the same few inches.

Of course the damage from pedestrians is not likely to cause as much of a problem to the landowner as will a field of foxhunting horse riders whose masters should ensure that a four-wheel drive vehicle follows the horses very closely, equipped with posts, barbed wire, sledge hammers and a couple of hefty people ready to repair immediately any damage caused by subscribers. A beagle pack will probably not need to go to these lengths (its followers mending their own problems as they occur) but, although we have already seen that a pack no longer requires the services of a field master,

Sunday morning volunteers repairing the damage made to a farmer's hedge during the previous day's sport

someone with the hunt's best interests at heart should remain with the majority of the followers and report any damage which cannot be repaired as soon as it occurs. It will be an unusual pack that never has a few supporters visiting the kennels the day after hunting has taken place, especially on a Sunday morning when much of the work for the week is carried out by keen volunteers, and so it should be an easy matter to gather up enough fence posts, staples and manual labour to go out and make right any damage caused the preceding day.

No one, whether they be directly concerned with the hunt or merely casual supporters, should ever forget at any time that they are enjoying their sport due to the kindness and indulgence of land-owners and farmers, without whose support their beagling could not continue. Yet however well it tries, a pack cannot go through life without causing upset at some time or another. The landowner may allow hounds to visit in November, thinking that as hares are generally to be found in the open areas of arable fields a meet will not disturb his carefully preserved pheasant stocks (unlike foxhounds who will need to draw his coverts to find a fox). He will

It is important to realise that beagling depends entirely on the goodwill of landowners and their tenants, and a few minutes spent in their company will often pay dividends when it comes to planning future meet cards

not be pleased to learn from his head gamekeeper that 'the beagles ran riot on deer and coursed it through East Wind Wood, disturbing a thousand pheasants which I had been keeping for the big shoot on Saturday . . .' It is better, therefore, for the huntsman or master to apologise immediately, even if it means that he needs to part with the pound coins in his breeches, promising a follow-up visit the next day. A bottle of whisky and an explanation the following day will probably prevent the keeper from mentioning the incident to his employer and it is unlikely that hounds following a strong scent will have caused any lasting effect — a fact which even the keeper will have to admit the next day when the pheasants appear on his feed rides as usual.

Most beaglers are a friendly bunch and so it is probably not necessary to mention that they should make a point of stopping and talking to anyone who is obviously responsible for the ground over which they are hunting, commenting on how well the newly planted corn looks or how expertly a particular piece of hedge has been laid or, to the keeper, that rumour has it that he is enjoying a good season with plenty of pheasants being put over the guns. Even if this is not the case, he is unlikely to admit it but the fact that someone is interested in his job will be received favourably.

From experience it seems that most masters have no objection to members of the field bringing out their pet dogs for a bit of exercise, provided of course that they are kept under control at all times. This is best achieved if they are kept on a lead and then there can be no temptation for a dog to join the pack, put up a squatting hare, flush gamebirds or chase livestock, activities which will not endear the dog's owner to anyone.

Gates must be opened and closed, even in the depths of winter when there is unlikely to be any livestock in the fields, and the beagler should shut the gate even when it is obvious that there are more people wishing to use it. If they are close behind him, however, he could leave it open and shout. 'Gate, please!' to the next group, making sure that at least one of them has heard his call and has acknowledged it. A gate left open without the farmer's knowledge, especially when it leads into a cornfield, is going to cause him no end of problems if he uses the track to drive cattle from one set of farm buildings to another or brings in sheep from another part of the farm as lambing time approaches.

Sheep which are obviously in lamb should be given a wide berth

The wrong way to use a gate! This one, being fully operational, should have been opened properly. When a gate is impossible to open, it should be climbed with care at its strongest point which is near the hinges, and *not* at the latch end *(Regina Arnold)*

by members of the field. Being notoriously panicky animals, a flock which takes fright and bunches together, bumping and jostling each other in the process, could well result in a few aborting. In fact it is probably much better for the master to avoid fixing a meet anywhere in the vicinity of sheep from Christmas onwards.

Following by car

There will always be a certain section of the hunt who, through choice or age and infirmity, follow the beagles by car. Although they are on the public highway and as such are governed by the rules of the road, they still have a certain responsibility towards the hunt. For instance, when hounds meet at a place which cannot cope with great numbers of vehicles, an effort should be made to park well away from the venue. This may seem a little unfair to members who have followed hounds all their lives and who now cannot walk any distance; in such cases a caring master should be able to organise a parking space close to the hound van. After all, it will probably be the only opportunity that these people have of seeing hounds at close quarters. For the rest, however, they should abide by the master's wishes in order not to spoil the day's sport: give the hounds a little leeway when they move off from the meet, switch off their engines when the pack is near and, perhaps just as important, remember to contribute to the 'cap'.

It will be unlikely that car followers will turn or otherwise head the hare, a crime which may be unwittingly carried out by foot followers and one which they should make every effort to avoid. On occasions, if the hare is leading hounds on to forbidden ground or towards potential danger in the shape of a railway or motorway, the whippers-in may have no alternative but to turn her deliberately. Otherwise she should be left to run her own course. In an effort to get a better view, followers might run towards a hedge only to find the hunted hare has doubled back on herself and is now coming to meet them. In such circumstances the field should stand still and try not to distract her. It is probably not necessary for them to throw themselves to the ground or crouch down, as such sudden movements are more likely to confuse the animal than would a statuesque pose through which both hare and hounds can run without ever being aware of the people's presence.

If the meet is being held on ground which borders that hunted by another pack, it is quite permissible for hounds to follow a line into their country and if, after a good hunt, they manage to kill it, so much the better. There is certainly no need to turn hounds in that situation. If, on the other hand, hounds pursue a hare into neighbouring country and then lose it, hounds must not under any circumstances draw a fresh hare whilst still in that country.

Scenting conditions

Weather conditions will have an effect on the day's hunting. Whilst a large field is all to the good from the point of view of the subscription list, it can cause problems of the kind already mentioned. On a wet, windy and cold day, however, all but the staunchest of supporters will probably stay at home, leaving the hunt staff to decide whether or not it is worth taking hounds out. Scenting and weather seem to be closely connected. Despite the many volumes written on the subject of scent by such acknowledged experts as Peter Beckford and Tom Smith, the whole thing continues to be something of a mystery but one point on which all 'experts' agree is that the behaviour of the quarry is very different on a poor scenting day than it is on a day when the ground holds a good scent.

It is probably easier to try and describe the weather conditions which will not produce a good scent than it is to describe those that will. A famous maxim of Beckford's was: 'Take not out your hounds on a windy day'. He probably meant to imply that any ground moisture, which is necessary for holding scent, would have been blown away. However, I think that most huntsmen would wish to change that maxim to: 'Take not out your hounds on a cold, frosty, snowy day'.

They would mention frost for a different reason from that of the foxhunting fraternity who would also think twice before hunting in such conditions. The concern of the latter would not be merely the lack of scent but also the well-being of their horses. A horse jumping a fence and landing wrongly on hard ground could injure itself severely and be out of action for the rest of the season or, worse, possibly be of no use on the hunting field for the rest of its life. It should be made clear at this stage that the type of frost being discussed is not the slight overnight affair which, as it thaws, will often improve scenting conditions as the day progresses, but the sort which is usually found after Christmas and the New Year and which lingers for days on end, working its way deeper and deeper into the soil. If snow then falls on top, not only is scenting guaranteed to be non-existent but, like the foxhunter's horse, continuous running over such ground does the hounds no good whatsoever. Before long there will be several members of the pack showing signs of lameness due to sprained tendons or pulled claws and it is not uncommon for a hound to lose a toe completely.

During a prolonged period of inactivity brought about by several days or weeks of snow and frost, it may be that the master and huntsman feel that they should take the hounds out purely to give them a bit of exercise and prevent them from going 'soft'. If a meet is arranged in such a case, then on this rare occasion the hunt staff need not concern themselves unduly with the subscribers and followers. There is no point in encouraging a large field to come along when they know in their heart of hearts that the meet will be a complete waste of time. The staff should not be influenced in their decisions by the enquiries to the kennels as to whether or not they are going to hunt as advertised on the card. When, as will inevitably happen, they are told that 'the so-and-so beagles haven't missed a day so far because of the weather', they must bite their tongue and keep the welfare of hounds in their mind at all times. After all, even though it may be a neighbouring pack of which they are speaking, weather conditions in country only a few miles away could be quite different.

Hunting a pack of hounds would be a great deal easier if there was never any wind but wind does have the advantage of blowing away any early morning mist and fog, although strangely enough the scent often seems to be quite good in these conditions — possibly due to the fact that the ground is warmer than the air and also because the ground is moist.

It is also evident, from watching hounds and taking note of the experiences of various huntsmen, that what starts out as a screaming scent on grassland, for instance, will often change as a hare takes hounds across a ploughed field or into marshy ground. The explanation put forward in such circumstances is that the grassland could be warmer than the air at the same time that the other type of ground is cooler. Conversely, it could be expected that scenting will be poor when these conditions are reversed and the air is warmer than the ground.

Dung spreading: an operation not conducive to a good day's sport when scenting may already be patchy *(Regina Arnold)*

Shooting readers, especially those with experience on the grouse moors, will know how poor scent is for the gundog when the ground is very dry and there is a lot of warm sunshine, especially when the heather is in full bloom and the pollen kills any chance the dog may have of picking up any scent at all — a fact borne out by many packs of beagles on their return from Northumberland, the Lake District, Exmoor and the like after their annual September sojourn mentioned earlier. 'Good weather, plenty to drink, but the scenting . . .!'

At times there are certain features likely to spoil a run on an otherwise good scenting day, the most obvious being when livestock such as cattle, sheep, gamebirds and dogs have crossed the hare's scent before hounds get to it. Bracken, dead leaves, and a field of kale or some other strongly scented crop are some more, if rather less obvious ones, whilst artificial fertilisers, chemicals and recent dung-spreading activities have also been found to be detrimental to the day's sport.

Many huntsmen lay claim to having a pack of hounds which can follow the scent of a hare along a tarmac road, a surface not normally known for holding a good scent. Apart from the obvious dangers in allowing hounds to hunt along a road in all but the quietest areas, I suspect that what they have in fact got is one good, reliable hound which may just be able to own the line and the rest of the pack are being carried along by his capabilities and cry. However, perhaps on a wet road, uncluttered by car exhaust fumes, the pack can follow the scent for a short distance before the hare leads them back to more productive ground.

Before leaving this complex and little understood subject, it is worth suggesting that the casual observer should watch how the huntsman changes his methods of hunting on a poor scenting day. Obviously there will be more work for him to do, casting his hounds at a check or working them to a view, and the worse the scent the more important it is that the huntsman should cheer on and encourage his leading hounds whenever they do manage to get away, for not only will there probably be less cry from them but also the pack will tend to split more easily. Before long, however, the follower will come to realise that the best huntsman of the day does not belong to this or that particular pack but is the average well-bred beagle, on whose nose and stamina the whole sport is based.

3
A HOUND TO HUNT THE HARE

How beagling evolved

The Royal Rock Beagles, whose country lies south-west of the River Mersey, were founded in 1845 and have the distinction of being the oldest pack of beagles still in existence anywhere in the world. Their formation is seen to be the beginning of the revival of beagling which has continued to the present day. Although to begin with the sport took off very slowly, with one or two hunts being formed in Surrey, south Middlesex and parts of Kent, by 1891 it was considered necessary to create the Association of Masters of Harriers and Beagles with the object of maintaining stud books and running the annual hound show at Peterborough. Four years later, in 1895, the Royal Rock was one of eighteen packs recognised by the association. Ninety-two years on things are very different and today there are ninety packs of beagles and twenty-eight packs of harriers recognised by the association, with a further eight packs of bassets and harehounds under the jurisdiction of the Masters of Basset Hounds Association.

Hunting the hare with hounds did not originate in the mid-nineteenth century, however, and it known that at least four hundred years before the birth of Christ the Greeks were using scenting hounds in order to pursue the hare. These hounds were very slow and their methods of hunting were very different from what we see today. The idea was not for the hounds to catch the hare but for them to drive it towards nets positioned over the 'runs' which the huntsman thought his quarry was most likely to use.

In Ancient Greece hounds were used not to catch the hare, but to drive it towards nets and a hidden huntsman; this illustration appears on a phial in the British Museum

Until the arrival in this country of the Normans, hares were considered by the nobility to be unworthy of hunting; the ordinary people, who it seems did not have much else going for them, were allowed to catch a hare by whatever means they had available. At first, the Normans preferred to hunt the deer and imposed many forest laws in order to preserve them but, as the wild woodland deer became less in number and harder to hunt, deer parks were set up and men employed to preserve the stocks. These then grew so large that it was once again an easy matter for the barons to enjoy the chase without too much effort. Poaching was of course a serious crime, punishable by death, but the ordinary man was all right: he still had his sport from the hare.

The hare was to be found both in open woodlands and in fields, neither of which were necessary for deer once the parks had been established, and the hare's habit of running in a circle once put up soon made hunting very popular with the young who liked the thrill of the hunt and the elderly who could watch hounds at work from a suitable vantage point without ever moving. Eventually, despite the predilection of the Norman kings for hunting the deer, the hare came to be regarded as the finer quarry of the two.

Edward Plantagenet, second Duke of York, was one of the greatest of all writers on sport. In his book *The Master of Game* he described what he considered to be the proper way of taking a hare with hounds and, although it was written between 1406 and 1413, the format for hare hunting as we know it in the twentieth century was beginning to emerge. The work of the hounds was still very slow by modern standards and there is an account of a day's hunting with Sir Roger de Coverley's hounds, at the end of which the hare was picked up alive only 8 yards in front of the pack which had been hunting her for almost as many hours. Had there been any kind of speed attached to the hunt, no hare could have remained alive after such a long time and the quality of a hunt was obviously judged by the amount of sport a hare could give rather than a distance from point to point or the length of run without a check.

All this time a hound was a hound and the type of hound would be the same regardless of whether the pack was kept to hunt deer, hare, fox or boar. By the 1550s hound breeds had become classified according to the size of quarry which they were most likely to hunt; thus the larger hounds became 'buck' and 'boar' hounds whilst the smaller breeds, kept only for hunting rabbits and hares, were called, in French, *bègle*, which over the years was anglicised to 'beagle'. In no way could these breeds be compared to our modern beagle, however, but they remain an important link in the evolutionary chain that produced foxhounds, harriers and (unlikely as it may seem) some types of terrier, where these were used in order to give nose and tongue. This would undoubtedly account for the hound colour of both the fox and wire-haired terriers.

Documents prove that the beagle was around and very popular in the time of Henry VIII, possibly due to the newly created open areas of countryside brought about by the felling of many pieces of woodland in order to provide timber during the Restoration period of history. Many of these areas became suitable for hare hunting. About this time, too, hare hunting began to descend back down the social hierarchy from the pedestal on which it had found itself and was the principal sport of squires and farmers who kept a few couples of mixed hounds on the farm and took them out whenever they liked. Before long, yeoman farmers and other individuals who could not perhaps afford to finance a full pack of hounds by themselves took to keeping just one or two couples and then arranging meets amongst themselves, to which all the hounds were brought and hunted by one of the owners. These 'scratch' or 'trencher' packs brought the sport even more within the reach of the ordinary person and, because of the wider interest taken in the breeding of hounds, a particular type would be bred, suitable for the country over which it was to hunt.

Before the sixteenth century when the breeds became classified, the only mention in literature was of a 'hound' suitable for hunting every form of quarry but records show that the first known pack of harriers in Britain was established by Sir Elias de Midhope in 1260 and that it hunted vast areas of what is now south Yorkshire. The Penistone Harriers existed for over five hundred years and for much of that time the masters were the Wilsons of Broomhead Hall. This type of large, slow-moving harrier was by now being crossed with the beagle in order to get as much bone and stamina in as small a frame as possible. Although this had the added advantage of improving the cry of hounds, it led to individuals being too fast for the remainder of the pack who did nothing but run, encouraged by the cry of the leading hounds, and never once had the chance of putting their noses down in order to own the scent. On the credit side, those hounds which did use their noses seemed to stick to a scent better than did the taller breeds of hound and, as the countryside became

Griffon Vendeen

70

Fauve de Bretagne

more and more enclosed, were more suited to dashing through hedgerows. The follower could also have a choice in the coat of his beagle, there being both the rough or wire-haired and the smooth-haired varieties.

The harrier still had its supporters, especially in the west and south-west of the country where a large, well-built hound with the head and shoulders of a mastiff and mottled, pied or liver-coloured was favoured. They were followed on foot as the ground was, at that time, too heavy to ride a horse across but, as irrigation drained the land and better cultivation improved the soil, eventually a lighter, faster hound, more like the modern harrier, evolved. It was known as the Southern hound, not because it originated in southern England but because it came from France where the hunting of the hare was also gaining in popularity as more and more of the less wealthy took to hunting on foot and required a slower type of hound, still with a good nose and strong enough to be able to cope with the local terrain, which at certain times of the year was impassable by normal means.

A hound which fitted all these requirements was found in the basset (meaning low set or dwarfed) order of French hound sizes. Whilst there were originally several types of basset, only four varieties now remain — two smooth-coated and two rough-haired — and these are the Griffon Vendeen, Fauve de Bretagne, Bleu de Gascogne and Artesian Normand. Their forebears resulted from a genetic freak in the sixteenth century when puppies of normal-sized French staghounds began to develop retarded limbs. In all other aspects they were normal and, purely out of curiosity, these small

71

Bleu de Gascogne

Artesian Normand

hounds were kept and mated together until they began to breed true to type. It was to be another hundred years before they appeared in this country and, in the meantime, the beagles had fallen on hard times probably due to the great improvements in the development of the harrier and the rapidly increasing interest in the 'new' sport of foxhunting which, it seems, had become accepted as a sport far superior to hare hunting.

Both the harriers and the foxhounds were now being bred by experts with a particular goal in mind. Blood lines and pedigrees were kept and the working ability of a hound was watched very closely. By means of line breeding, some careful inbreeding and outcrossing with other hunts, the owners of what have become the most prestigious of today's hound packs bred an even pack with a good turn of speed and noses to match. Many masters began to draft their hounds with other hunts in order to achieve the qualities that both were looking for. Harriers were brought to a state of perfection by a repetition of crosses between the beagle, the foxhound and earlier colloquial breeds of harrier types such as the Southern and Western which, according to the writings of the famous Parson John Russell, were themselves descended from the staghound. Gradually individual blood lines began to mingle into the one breed but some

The modern-day Gascony Harrier, the ancestors of which were used to dilute the blood of our earlier, heavier breeds in order to produce a faster hunting hound

packs deliberately held on to the older type of hound, notably the Holcombe Harriers who still hunt the areas between Liverpool and Blackburn and who, up until World War II at least, could show a hound with traces of the Southern and Gascony harrier in their make-up. Today, their hounds are no different from any of the other twenty-seven packs of harriers hunting in this country, the change having been brought about by the subscribers and followers who compared their hounds with others and decided that they were too slow for the horses.

Horse breeding also took a part in deciding the future of the beagles. Beagling was too boring; any action was very slow and certainly did not require the services of the part thoroughbred hunter which had been developed throughout the previous century by private landowners in order to keep up with the faster foxhounds. Better, then, to use these hounds and horses and hunt the fox over ground such as was found in areas of Leicestershire where it was impossible to grow corn due to the poor clay soil and so a good run over large estates composed only of grassland and hedges was guaranteed. Small coverts and spinneys containing thick, warm undergrowth such as gorse were planted in an effort to encourage a fox and once it had been pushed out from this cover by the hounds it had no alternative but to run over open country in order to reach the protection of the next wood.

The majority of foxhunters preferred these gorse coverts to big woodland with its heavy rides. Even when the cover had grown tall and hollow, it was still possible to find a leash or two of foxes which would provide a good run.

Another point in favour of foxhunting was the fact that, because the fox was nothing more than vermin, outsiders could ride over private ground in its pursuit whereas the game laws then in force confined the right to hunt or shoot any form of game (which, of course, included hares) to landowners only and thus the ordinary people of the land were excluded.

Not wishing to miss any of the excitement, many of the harrier packs decided to start hunting the fox, or at least did not worry whether hounds put up a hare or a fox. Of those owners of private packs which did remain faithful to the hare, their harriers by this time were only foxhounds in miniature anyway. The standard height was around 18 inches, which was considered about the right size for hunting the hare, and these lighter hounds seemed to possess much greater stamina than those heavily built Gascons and Talbots which the eighteenth-century gentry had kept.

In 1903 there were around 150 harrier packs, many of which have since been disbanded, changed to hunting the fox or, like the Sandhurst and Colne Valley Harriers at some time during the early part of this century, turned their kennels over to beagles.

What had been happening to the beagle throughout this period is uncertain and there is very little mention of their development in any writings of the time. Blaine, in his *Encyclopaedia of Rural Sports* published in 1840, refers to several varieties of beagle, two of which were the wire-haired (probably descended from the Welsh hounds) and the smooth-coated mentioned earlier. The breed had been recognised by the Kennel Club in 1873 and it seems the pocket beagle was beginning to attain a certain popularity. They were never more than 10 inches high and eventually bred true to type. In the *Sportsman's Cabinet* written in 1804, it was noted that '. . . the late Col Hardy had once a collection of this diminutive tribe amounting to ten or twelve couple, which were always carried to and from the field of glory in a large pair of panniers slung across a horse; small as they were . . . they could invariably keep a hare at all her shifts to escape them, and finally worry, or rather tease her to

'Truelove', a black-and-tan beagle typical of the late nineteenth/early twentieth centuries

death'. The life of that particular pack was apparently brought to a rather sudden end when the kennels were broken into and the hounds and the panniers were stolen, never to be recovered. Other packs of pocket beagles seemed to be more fortunate and the interest in them continued up until World War I.

Slowly, what is now seen as the standard beagle began to reappear, until the revival which saw the birth of the Royal Rock ensured the future of both beagles and beagling.

At the same time the basset hound appeared on these shores. Although Sir Everett Millais is presumed by most people to have been the man largely instrumental in introducing the hound, it was in fact Lord Galway in 1866 who was responsible and it was nearly ten years later that Millais built up a kennel of bassets and began to breed them seriously. In an effort to avoid a narrow breeding base he introduced a bloodhound outcross, effectively rejuvenating the breed and forming the heavier, loose-skinned basset we see on the show benches today.

The basset was primarily brought into this country to see how it coped with hunting the hare, however, and in 1891 Major Godfrey Heseltine and his brother Geoffrey founded the Walhampton hunt with freshly imported hounds from France which dominated both the show ring and hunting field for nearly thirty years. Soon, as with many breeds, the show dog began to differ greatly from those which were kept only for hunting and, as masters of hunting packs were the largest kennel owners and obviously bred hounds which could both stand a day's hunting and catch hares, the Masters of Basset Hounds Association was formed with the Master of the Wroxton Abbey Basset Hounds, Lord North, elected as its first president. The club founded by Galway, Onslow and Millais died a natural death as breeders began to insist on peculiarities in type which caused the animal to lose its natural hunting ability. Also instrumental in the termination of the club was the outbreak of World War I when breeding, showing and hunting were severely affected, so much so that only nine hounds were registered during the war years.

After the death of Major Heseltine in 1932 his pack was sold off and some of these hounds provided a means of reviving the breed when crossed with imported Artesian Normands. The fresh interest created resulted not only in the reforming of the Basset Hound Club in 1954 but also an extension of their objectives in the form of a working branch. From this arose the Albany Basset Hounds, a properly constituted pack with kennels, hunt staff, uniforms and followers, also recognised by the Masters of Basset Hounds Association with its own registered country situated in the triangle between Melton Mowbray, Stamford and Spalding. These hounds were also Kennel Club registered and proved that the heavy-bodied type of basset could, in fact, hunt the hare successfully. They are of course hunted on foot and, not being fast, this is as it should be: the hares which they catch are caught as a result of a fair hunt and good houndwork.

The only exception to this was the Brancaster pack of bassets, now unfortunately no longer in existence, which was hunted by Miss Ena Adams who felt that, as the country was predominantly plough, she should hunt from horseback and she gradually bred a pack of bassets which were up to 18 inches high, standing on straight legs rather than the more usual crooked, Queen Anne style. With such a description, it is difficult to imagine this pack being any different from a kennel of harriers, similar in height and stature and (with the exception of the Wensleydale Harriers) also hunted from horseback.

Any developments in the breeding of the harehound, whether harrier, beagle or basset, seem to have ceased by World War II and so the basset remained in its various forms, being all things to all men. The harrier, however, set several standards. The more orthodox packs kept to the idea of the hound being nothing more than a foxhound in miniature and, as a result, the majority of today's packs kennel a beautifully level group of good-coloured hounds which are capable of hunting the country in which they are recognised. Once again, the hounds which appear to last the longest, and go out on the greatest number of days in the season, are the lighter-built breeds varying between 18 and 21 inches at the shoulder, well within any standards set as the accepted norm.

The beagle today

The size of the modern beagle is largely a decision left to the masters of individual packs. The limit of 16 inches at the shoulder is imposed by the Association of Masters of Harriers and Beagles at their annual hound show held at Peterborough, but there are several packs hunting the hare which contain hounds taller than this. For a long time beagles between 14 and 15 inches in height have been accepted as being the most suitable size for an average country where plough and grass alternate and they can show consistently good sport even when the hunting conditions are appalling. Larger hounds are used very successfully by those hunts which meet frequently in country which is open and hilly with large expanses of rough cover such as heather and bracken. It is obvious that these areas can be punishing for a smaller hound but the great disadvantage with these heavier beagles, from the follower's point of view at least, is that they are often so fast that it is almost impossible to follow the hunt at close quarters. The followers of a smaller pack should, if they are reasonably fit, be able to keep up with hounds and see most of the run. It is the opinion of most experienced masters that the smaller the hound, the closer they hunt to the line of the hare, but where stone walls and deep ditches abound the small beagle would be tired out before getting to terms with the hare. The larger hounds can often cause problems to the whippers-in and are

A level pack: the Sandhurst beagles with huntsman Michael Jackson. Even though 'a good horse is never a bad colour', a pack which is not only of a level size, but also more or less uniform in colour, is an attractive sight

said to be more difficult to stop when, for instance, they are heading towards woodland containing deer or pheasants or towards the obvious dangers associated with roads and railways, than would be the case with hounds of 14 inches.

Whatever size the actual hounds may be, the pack as a whole must be level if it is to have any chance of hunting together without a leader running well in advance and the stragglers trailing along the line at least a field behind. If such a situation arises, probably the only thing for the masters and huntsman to do is to draft those hounds which consistently hunt far in front or lag behind to another pack which has slower or faster hounds.

Whatever the breed, a hound to hunt the hare must possess speed, size, nose and in general an overall ability to hunt. If these hounds happen to show well on the flags, that is certainly a desirable bonus, and whilst a hound can be persuaded to show itself by good handling (a doubtful neck, for example, being shown by the huntsman holding a biscuit about knee height) nevertheless the basic formation has to be there in the first place with good, sloping shoulders and a reasonable length of neck. Of course there will be slight differences between dog and bitch but in both cases the neck should be free from too heavy an appearance.

Points of the beagle

A good length of muzzle will give the beagle the traditional hound look and, accompanied by the dark, benevolent eyes, goes a long way to explaining the animal's appeal. A serious fault which should not be encouraged in any breed of dog is that of an undershot or overshot jaw which will show with increasing regularity if such hounds are used for breeding. Teeth should be strong and even.

Running from the neck to the chest, there must be a good spring to the ribs so that they are 'deep', giving plenty of room for the lungs and heart. This is perhaps a beagle's most necessary qualification, providing that his nose is good enough to keep him on the line. It is often said that a flat-sided hound is as good as one with well sprung ribs, but good ribs are generally a sign of staying power. The chest should then extend an inch or so below the point of the elbows which, provided that they are set square, neither turned out nor pinched in, will ensure that the forelegs are straight. On any type of hound the straightness of the leg will be immediately appa-

Aldershot Fireman '82. A beautifully conformed dog hound with exceptionally straight forelegs

rent to even the most uninformed of observers; if the bone of the foreleg is then carried right down into the foot, so that there is not the slightest appearance of an ankle, the thickness might seem at first to be larger than is necessary but when one considers that this thickness and length will help to prevent any jarring at the shoulder when landing, the sense of such breeding will be appreciated.

A good underline will carry the eye to the hind legs — which provide the necessary propelling power when the beagle is hunting at full pelt — and if these are coupled with strong hocks and hindquarters, so much the better.

The stern should arise from a perfectly level spine, set at right angles and giving the impression of being thick and powerful at the base. When in the kennels or on the flags it should be carried straight and perpendicular, or with the faintest trace of a sickle-type curve. The back itself, provided that it is muscular and the flesh shows as being ever so slightly curved, will as a matter of course be strong and capable of supporting a hound throughout the day.

These physical characteristics are of paramount importance and, combined with all the other essential qualities of the beagle (stamina, nose, tongue and drive), should be the ultimate aim of every master and huntsman if they intend to give the field some first-class hunting.

A lack of stamina is very often responsible for the development of skirting. Without stamina, certain hounds soon begin to look for ways and means of cutting corners and anticipating the movements of the intended quarry and of the more reliable members of the pack. For this reason, if no other, it is a mistake to keep more entered hounds in a kennel than are absolutely essential: the amateur member of hunt staff, unable to keep a constant eye on his charges, will find it impossible to tell which of his hounds are capable of standing up to a day's hunting and which are not, and over the years a line of constitutionally weak beagles may be perpetuated.

Closely conected with stamina is drive, which should not be confused with physical speed. If speed is bred into a hound beyond a certain point, other attributes are bound to suffer; after all, a hound is only as good as its nose and there can be no advantage in breeding fast limbs which will often make a beagle overrun the scent of a hare, causing many unnecessary checks during the hunting day. The inability to own a line will also affect the individual hound's cry which, with an excessive increase in speed, must be expected to decrease. Drive may then be defined as the ability to get over the ground as quickly as possible under the existing scenting conditions and not to their exclusion. Nowadays, the merit of a hunt is judged by the amount of time without a check but it should not be forgotten that hare hunting is a sport, judged (if that is the right word) by the hounds' hunting ability and their ways of dealing with a difficult scent.

The importance of tongue cannot be overemphasised. If one asks the supporters of basset hounds why they follow their particular pack, they will invariably give as one of the reasons the fact that the basset has the most beautiful cry of any hound. Whatever the breed, when the pack is in full cry the sound not only adds to the followers' enjoyment but also helps them and the hunt staff to keep in touch when hounds are temporarily out of sight. A good huntsman will be able to recognise some individual hounds by their voices alone and, if they are known to be reliable and consistent in their capabilities, this will give him a good indication as to what is happening over the hill.

Individual preference

Followers of the basset would also say that their hounds are ideal for hunting the hare and would hold them in higher esteem than the beagle because of their ability to follow a scent which is several hours old. Indeed it was said of the old stamp of basset that one could take the pack out hunting, chase the hare all day, call off the hunt when either hounds or huntsmen got tired and place a marker peg in the ground where they last owned the scent, returning to the kennels secure in the knowledge that, at some convenient time the following day, the pack could be brought back to the peg and laid on the line where hunting had ceased the previous evening! Perhaps this is carrying the praise of their scenting powers a little to far but it serves to illustrate the basset's wonderful nose and its tenacity on a catchy scent or a dying hare.

Most bassets have either been crossed with beagles or are bred almost as tall in order to be able to hunt as fast. Some packs also contain a mixture of beagle and basset, thereby ensuring that all the varying hound qualities are brought together. I cannot imagine that such a pack would hunt close enough to enable one to cover the group with the proverbial tablecloth but have to admit that I have not seen such a pack out on a hunting day and so should possibly reserve judgement. Generally speaking, however, those packs labelled as bassets will probably be found to contain the traditional short-legged, long-eared and long-bodied type of hound whilst those who prefer to call their pack harehounds will arrive at the meet with several couple of the longer-legged, shorter-eared hound which stands at around 15 to 16 inches at the shoulder and is much heavier in the bone than the average beagle. Legs straight and strong no doubt help the likes of the East Lincs Harehounds whose country, situated between Boston and Cleethorpes, has more than its fair share of heavy ploughland.

Harehounds of a very different stamp, hunting very different country but nevertheless just as capable of hunting the hare as any of the other packs and types previously mentioned, are the Hydfer Harehounds privately owned and kennelled between Dr D. G. Rees and Mr David Evans. Their country is loaned from the Glyn Celyn Beagles and has basically the same borders as the Sennybridge Foxhounds. Dr Rees, who hunted hounds whilst living in Northern Ireland, where many hounds are trencher fed and each owner is convinced that his own couple of beagles are the mainstay of the pack, was determined to reintroduce the system to his part of Wales but found that followers would not travel even a few miles down the road although they constantly asked when hounds would be visiting their land and would have been very insulted if the pack met without first coming in for whisky and welshcakes and returning for tea when finishing.

Although historically the country is more suited to harriers or foxhounds, Dr Rees's small pack has, since 1967, contained blood mixtures of the Kerry beagle, basset, Welsh hound, small harriers, the Southern and blue-mottled hound and, perhaps most surprisingly, the bloodhound. In its purebred form the latter, although possessing an excellent nose, is most unsuited to hunting the hare for a long period of time and unless it is at all times almost on top of the quarry it will soon lose interest. Once outcrossed, however, it forms a very useful addition to the pack but still cannot be totally trusted on the open mountains where sheep abound all year round. Indeed, probably the only hounds that can be so trusted are those derived from the Welsh hound, which over the years has almost without exception become sheepwise.

The ultimate aim in such apparently haphazard breeding is to achieve hounds with unfailing scenting abilities. Then, in Dr Rees's opinion, it will be the quality of hunting which is of utmost importance and not the quantity of hounds in the pack. Accuracy in the Hydfer pack, when only six or seven couple of hounds are taken out for the day and can still hunt a hare on a fair basis after the manner of Sir Roger de Coverley, is to be admired and, maybe, emulated.

Colouring and coats

The Hydfer owns hounds which still show traces of blue mottle in their colouring but any hound colour suits the beagle; white, black and tan is probably the most popular combination but it was not that long ago that hounds were bred a certain colour in order to be in fashion, irrespective of the personal thoughts of individual masters and huntsmen. It was more usual to find that being fashionable was more important in the best of the foxhound kennels but it was inevitable that some beagle packs would follow suit.

A favourite colour for foxhounds was for many years the Belvoir tan, with little or no white on the top half of the body and legs. A good hound can never be a bad colour and it is impossible for its hunting ability to be affected by pigmentation but when the sixth Duke of Rutland tried to include light-coloured hounds in his pack subsequent breeding trials found that the resultant entry had none of the stamina of the dark tan. With today's more thorough knowledge on hound breeding, we know that the lack of stamina was due to the fault of the blood from which the light-coloured hounds were bred rather than to their colour. During the same period, other prestigious kennels were full of light-coloured hounds which were showing excellent sport and so it was obvious, even then, that the lack of drive and stamina had nothing at all to do with their colouration.

Fortunately, the rather silly fashion fad was short lived in all kennels whether they contained foxhounds, harriers, bassets or beagles. Nowadays dark tan, hare pie, lemon and white and Dr Rees's blue tick all have their admirers but, whatever the colour, the stern in all breeds should ideally be tipped with white.

As the basset emerged and showed that it was capable of hunting the hare, its admirers were rather strict in laying down the law and stipulated that '. . . the colour should be black, white and tan, the head, shoulders and quarters a rich tan, and black patches on the back. They are sometimes hare pied . . .' However, as we have seen, the basset has changed, sometimes out of recognition, and, within reason, anything goes now.

Drawing for a hare *(Geoff Burch)*

Of course the colour of hounds is largely a matter of the master's preference but, like the size of the hound, the colour may depend to some extent on the country over which they hunt. Although a beagle should never need to appear in the woodlands, a pack which hunts predominantly woodland country is most easily followed if they contain a light-coloured proportion which can be seen against the normally dark backdrop.

As for the coat, in any hound of good breeding and under correct kennel management it will, as a matter of course, be fine, close and short, with the ears feeling fine in texture and the hair silky to the touch, with an overall gloss similar to that found on a good-quality horse.

Sometimes, despite the concentrated efforts of all those concerned, certain characteristics which are desired by a particular pack fail to materialise and, for one reason or another, the resultant hound is not their idea of a hound to hunt the hare. Then there is no alternative but to draft.

Drafting hounds

A young hound should always be allowed its 'salad days' and there must be no hurry to draft a hound which is often merely a little slow in understanding what is required of it whilst out hunting but there is certainly no point in feeding hounds when they are never likely to further any future breeding policies.

There will always be a pack of harehounds looking for certain points which may be unfavourable to those which bred an individual, and each year there will always be at least one kennel which has suffered an unexpected loss due to accident or disease and which will obviously be very grateful for any hounds to help overcome the disaster.

Very often the best way to approach the problems of which hounds to draft is to remember that the ultimate aim is to achieve a level pack and then to decide on those animals which are harmful to the pack. Preference is sometimes given to the mute or nearly mute: an otherwise good hunting day can be ruined when a couple of hounds slip away silently, leaving the hunt staff with no idea as to

The draw *(Geoff Burch)*

their whereabouts. A harehound which is much faster than the remainder is also undesirable and is best removed, unless it is possible to breed only from these hounds and then select from the subsequent entry those which are always found at the front — in other words take hounds from the front every year. Another pack in another part of the country might find that the faster hound suits its requirements.

The dangers of holding on to skirters or those which refuse to draw have already been explained and they should also be added to the draft list, along with those which are not quite all they might be in make and shape.

These surplus hounds should never be offered for sale (at least in this country) and the Association of Masters of Harriers and Beagles recommends that its members should only draft unwanted hounds to other registered and recognised packs. At its 1958 annual general meeting the association approved the following resolution:

> With a view to maintaining and improving the quality of the blood registered in the Association's Stud Book, the Joint Committee urge upon Masters the importance of breeding only from those hounds who have proved themselves to be absolutely sound in their work.

Another way one pack can draft a hound in order to help a pack which is less fortunate is to offer as a brood bitch one who has come to the end of her hunting days and who, provided that she is not too old and has had a litter or two or pups earlier in her career, could prove a useful asset for a couple of seasons and a nucleus for a new line of breeding. This is an especially valid point now that, in the minds of many of today's breeders, a hound is finished as far as hunting is concerned after five or six seasons. Kept any longer than that, there seems to be the fear that they would be deemed slow and this would affect not only the pack's hunting ability but also the hunt's reputation. Several decades ago, many packs contained hounds which were eight, nine, ten or even more years old. However, there are many kennels where longevity is much sought after and where hounds are bred that still manage to keep their speed.

There is another, less desirable point which may cause a hound to be drafted to another hunt and that is sheep killing. An otherwise brilliant beagle should not necessarily be destroyed for this heinous crime but he should be immediately removed from the pack before he has a chance to pass on these habits to other members. There are packs which never see sheep from one year to the next and it may be possible for masters and huntsmen to draft a hound to such a hunt. Failings of this nature are more likely to occur during moorland hunting or when the pack is continually taken to meets situated on 'intake' land or secondary grazing where sheep are the only viable form of farming income. Then it is essential that hounds are absolutely steady as these active upland sheep often jump up from the peat hag immediately in front of the pack, but even then there is still the danger of a hound which is unavoidably left out after the day's hunting and which develops a taste for mutton. Sometimes it is possible for a young hound to be cured by tying it down along a passageway or at a gate and driving sheep uncomfortably close by or even over it, or confining it in a box with a ewe and her newly born lambs, but even then there is still the danger that the hound may come across a sheep trapped in wire or brambles and his interest may be rekindled as the sheep struggles and bleats in an effort to break free. Then it is only a matter of time before the beagle begins to bark at the sheep and attract a few young hounds who all get excited and pretty soon the fatal act is committed.

As far as entered drafts are concerned, these have always been regarded by most people with some suspicion — if they had been any good they would never have been drafted in the first place. However, this kind of swapping of hounds is in general an excellent way of ensuring the future well-being of any breed. With no expensive stud fees there is no need for the potential breeder to baulk from taking a bitch to the top dog in order to achieve the best, a fact which can only bode well for a hound to hunt the hare. Whether it be beagle, basset or harrier is a decision which can only be made by the follower but, whatever choice he makes, there is plenty of fun and exercise to be had from a day with the harehounds.

4

HARES: FACT AND FICTION

Every countryman knows the old saying that if one sees a hare in a field and it remains the same size as one gets closer, it is not a hare but merely a clod of earth. Only if it gets smaller is it likely to be a hare!

Despite this apparent difficulty, a sound knowledge and understanding of the hare's habits is very necessary if the newcomer to beagling wishes to get the best from his sport. To the huntsman such information is an absolute essential if he intends to show good sport and maintain the interest of his followers.

By understanding the hare's movements and its possible behaviour when being hunted by hounds, supporters who do not care to chase madly after the pack simply in order to find themselves back in the same place after a quarter of an hour's heart-stopping, energy-wasting exercise, can select for themselves a likely vantage point from which to watch the hunt unravel.

The hare's year

Traditionally, the mating season is given as the period between January and April but mild weather at Christmas time sometimes accounts for the fact that young leverets are to be found as early as January and late leverets are often met with as far into the year as November.

Recent research, carried out by various well-informed and eminently qualified individuals, proves and disproves many long-held theories about the hare's life style. For instance, 'boxing' was thought to be carried out only by the males as part of their attempts to achieve territory and a mate, giving rise to the 'mad March hare' syndrome, but in actual fact it is now known that a boxing hare is likely to be a female turning and defending herself from the unwanted attentions of the male. Since the doe is bigger and more powerfully built than the buck, the latter frequently has to suffer a rather rough passage before the time comes when the female is receptive and willing for consummation. When two hares are seen together in the early part of the year, therefore, they will probably be male and female, with the buck waiting for the doe to come on heat.

However, even during this important time of the hare's calendar there will probably be no determined fight for a certain territory and, providing that the chosen feeding areas are capable of supplying an adequate diet, many animals can live and reproduce on a relatively small acreage.

Hares are very promiscuous and there appears to be no permanent pairing; a doe is often served by two or three bucks in quick succession. Having said this, it is necessary to contradict the statement by pointing out that there is always the possibility that certain males are capable of developing a type of heirarchy with the most

A hare in its form, showing just how effective the pelage can be as a means of camouflage. How many members of the average beagling field would notice this particular animal before she noticed them? *(Geoff Burch)*

Male and female boxing; since the doe is bigger and more powerfully built, the buck frequently has to suffer a rather rough passage before a successful mating

prominent buck protecting his does from other males, but when males fight each other they will usually chase and bite rather than 'box'.

As we have already begun to see, boxing and mating procedures do not only occur in the early months of the year and it has been proved that such behaviour will also take place throughout the summer and early autumn. The reason why these activities are not so easily seen by the casual observer is due, in part, to the fact that the intimacies of mating take place in the early morning when all but the keenest watchers are still at home in bed.

Two to five seems to be the average number of leverets in a litter and, depending on the weather, the doe (who normally begins breeding at about a year old) can have three or four litters during the course of a season. Wet weather will, naturally, diminish her chances but, after a gestation period of around thirty days, the leverets are born.

Unlike many young mammals, they emerge from the mother's womb fully clothed, have their eyes open and are quite capable of using their legs to escape danger. For some reason not yet fully understood, however, they are loath to put their legs into action, preferring instead to rely on camouflage, and it is often possible to pick them up before they are frightened into action.

There is no doubt that the hare is an animal which evolution has well adapted to evade attacks from predators. Its eyes, large and brown, are set high in its skull and the head is flattened along the plane of the eye so that it is possible for it to see almost all the way round. However, owing to this eye positioning, the sight straight ahead is not thought to be all that wonderful, even though the large, horizontal pupils are capable of concentrating its vision when running at speed. Perhaps this is the real reason why hares prefer to squat and rely on their senses of hearing and smell rather than trust to their undoubted speed.

For a long time it was thought that shortly after birth the doe found a separate form for each of her young, carrying them to their new nurseries in her mouth in just the same way as a cat carries her kittens, and thereafter visiting them at night to suckle them. This is only partially correct and the recent research has shown that the litter stays in the form in which they were born for only a couple of days. After this, the leverets take themselves off to a suitable place and then it is up to the doe to locate her young. A clicking sound made by grinding the teeth was thought to be an alarm sound given off by the adults but it is now realised that the noise is used by the young to inform the parents of their whereabouts: when the doe is going to suckle her leverets, it is they that call to her and not the other way round.

Suckling is only likely to happen once every twenty-four hours but a single feed from the lactating mother seems to be sufficient for the leverets until they are weaned at three weeks to a month old.

The last litter of the season is luckier than their predecessors and there seems to be no hurry on the part of the doe to terminate her maternal duties, feeding the leverets much longer than would normally be expected. Therefore a female found lactating in winter is not necessarily nursing a newly born litter, and her death from hunting or shooting will not mean leaving leverets unable to fend for themselves.

Making a census

When one hare is seen in a field, it is safe to assume that there is a strong likelihood of another being hidden in the close vicinity, but a wholly accurate hare count or census is virtually impossible.

When it comes to planning the following season's meet card, however, some time spent by the hunt staff in assessing the hare stocks could prove advantageous and it is doubtful whether any conservationally minded landowner or farmer will object to a count being carried out.

There are several ways to go about it. Whereas brown hares are generally difficult to observe during daytime, at night when they are active their eyeshine makes them easy to see with a spotlight. The Game Conservancy, which studied the hare's life style in great detail for three years in the early part of this decade, found that the most successful method was to use a four-wheel-drive vehicle fitted with a 100 watt spotlight, the beam of which was swept round in a semicircular movement and the hares counted by using binoculars. Between thirty and forty sampling sites were selected on each estate and the best and most obvious period of the year in which to carry out a census was found to be during the beagling season, when vegetation in most crops was at its lowest.

The range at which a hare was visible varied from night to night because of autumnal mists and so, before and after each count, the length of the spotlight beam was measured by assessing the distance at which the observer could distinguish a one centimetre square of red reflective tape which simulated the reflection of a hare's eye.

Other, more traditional methods of counting animals in a given area work quite well but are more labour intensive and it is doubtful whether the keenest farmer or landowner will be pleased to allow a group of beaters on to his land to flush hares forward for men using counters. Two people holding a rope between them which is then allowed to brush the field surface however works well in flushing hares.

Whatever method is used, regular counts over the same area will be necessary in order to make a reasonable assessment and, as there will always be some animals not seen, it is probably safer to say that there are at least so many hares in an area rather than to 'guesstimate' and say that, as one half of the farm contains a certain number, then it follows that the other half will contain an approximately similar number. Hares are not normally distributed evenly across farmland but are aggregated.

Preferred ground and feeding areas

Hares prefer low, rolling ground and spend most of their lives in forms in the open. Of course their density and whereabouts on the

Typical hare country: dry, chalky soil with, in the foreground, a cereal crop. The dairy unit at the bottom of the track, and the herd in the middle distance, indicate that the ground surrounded by hedgerows is likely to be pasture. On the horizon a shelter belt of trees provides a windbreak for the hare, as well as a winter food source. From the point where the photograph was taken, going clockwise, it is possible for a hare to graze her way through all four seasons

ground depend mainly on the estate's farming methods and there can be no doubt that, since the early 1960s, the hare population has diminished as agriculture has become greatly intensified.

Diversified farms with small fields were found to be no longer economically viable and it was then not possible for the hare to be able to site its form in such a position so as to live in an area which gave easy access to all crops at all times of the year. Hares need a habitat which is suitable for both shelter and food and, since they are nocturnal, sheltering places (especially during the winter months) are frequented by day and feeding areas by night. Woodlands and to some extent long crops are generally used for shelter, whereas short crops and pasture are used as areas in which to feed.

The extraction of wooded areas and hedgerows and the increase in arable monoculture mean that it is less likely that the hare can remain in one form and still be able to move between the fields as crops develop or are replaced throughout the year.

Hares are wholly vegetarian and eat chiefly grasses and roots, and a home range of about 60 hectares should contain all that is necessary for an individual animal's year-round consumption.

As winter corn is available for around ten months of the year. It is a valuable crop during the more severe months and it will contain feed for the hare from its planting and emergence through to about March. After this the feed value is limited and it is used by the hare mainly as shelter cover. Spring corn and stubble turnips are of positive value in encouraging the hare; although they are only available for around four months of the year they can provide over a quarter of the food source in percentage terms.

Not only will the hare move from one crop to another depending on the time of year but its distribution will be significantly affected by livestock such as cattle and sheep. From what has gone before, it might be supposed that short grass would provide the ideal feeding medium and so it will, but only when the livestock has had its fill and been moved on to fresh fields. There is no doubt that hares are greatly disturbed by livestock and generally keep off areas heavily stocked with sheep or cattle. As the shepherd or herdsman moves his stock between field and paddock, hares shift their grazing patterns in order to make use of the vacated ground. Although stock rotation may temporarily disrupt the hares' grazing patterns, it is unlikely to reduce their available food seriously.

The possible effects of spraying

An over-use of certain herbicides on the autumn stubbles could have a detrimental effect on the hare population. However, this is unlikely on a dual-purpose farm which is managed sensibly, for when the hare has the full range of pasture, stubble crops and newly planted winter wheat to choose from there is no need for it to scratch a living from the autumn stubble.

Most sprays appear to be non-toxic with the exception of those which contain paraquat, notably Gramoxone. The notes and general guidance given in detail on all carefully produced sprays tell the farmer that the product is likely to prove fatal to all forms of livestock for at least twenty-four hours. (It is an interesting point, though probably not one of any real consequence, that the effect on

Spraying a healthy crop of wheat: a farming operation unlikely to upset the resident hare population. The general decline started long before the widespread use of herbicides and insecticides

hares is always mentioned.) But even Gramoxone is unlikely to cause much damage because at the time when it is used, that is immediately after harvest, hares will probably not be feeding on the stubble. In fact the decline in the hare population started long before the widespread use of herbicides and insecticides.

Other reasons for the hare's decline

What are the other reasons for the hare's decline? Of course there is likely to be a natural annual mortality in the autumn when the leverets begin to find life more difficult. There is no definite cause of death attributable in these cases and post-mortems on such hares find no obvious pesticide residues.

Some casualties found by keepers, farmers and landowners seem to have been perfectly fit and healthy but others are thin and obviously full of some form of viral infection, with the young of the year often covered in lesions, scab infections and parasites and suffering from coccidiosis and similar diseases.

An interesting point, born out by the recent research, is the fact that as the hare has declined then so too has predation on the hare increased. In particular, the number of foxes has increased since the early years of the 1960s. Perhaps this increase coincides with the lessening in numbers of gamekeepers situated around the country-side. In the interests of their game stocks, conscientious keepers will take every opportunity to rid the estate of predators, and foxes prove the most obvious danger. With wages rising and much shooting ground being taken over by groups of enthusiasts working on a do-it-yourself basis, there is often not the time to carry out as comprehensive a programme of predator control as when there is a full-time, professional keeper. Large acreages of shooting ground which used to provide employment for many keepers are now managed by one man and what hope does he have of controlling vermin when he has other, more important tasks such as collecting the eggs from the laying pen, incubation, and preparing the rearing field and release pens?

An analysis made of the diet of foxes on arable land seems to indicate that hares form a major component of their diet and it has been calculated that a breeding population of at least sixty-nine adult hares would be required to support one single fox family throughout the year. Those who fondly believe that the fox only eats earthworms, small mammals, vegetation and carrion would do well to study in detail the contents of a fox's droppings: by doing so they would probably be surprised to learn that hares, in an area where these are plentiful, form the major part of a fox's diet — higher even than gamebirds or rabbits, two species which have long been thought to contribute greatly towards the fox's dinner plate.

This feeding pattern though is more likely to occur during the summer months, say from April to September, as the vixens begin breeding and there are more mouths to feed. Most of the hares killed will be females taken either during or before they have had a chance to breed. It is also reasonable to assume that although the leverets are born fully clothed, open-eyed and ready to run, they will not do so if they can possibly avoid it. Instead they much prefer to lie in the form which they have chosen, and so close that it often requires a very keen eye to spot them. They will remain like this until the last possible moment and many true naturalists and countrymen can tell of the time that they have picked up a young leveret before it has made up its mind to move. If it is possible for a relatively clumsy human to do this, then it must be an easy matter for an experienced fox to do the same.

Around active breeding fox earths, hare remains containing the complete pelvic girdle have been found, very often with the hind limb bones still attached. These remains are probably produced by the activities of the cubs who, being unable to crack the bones, simply suck and rasp the meat from them. More proof, then, of the importance of hares in their diet. There can then be little doubt that the hare population will have a lower average survival rate when many foxes are present.

Predation on its own is, however, unlikely to be responsible for the recent decline in hare numbers. The Game Conservancy, reviewing its own research, feels that it is only one of three main factors, all of which, in combination, probably account for some of the decline. One of the other reasons suggested is a succession of poor breeding seasons which meant that the exceptionally high numbers of hares around during the early 1960s declined rapidly. The third and most important factor is, in the opinion of the Game Conservancy, 'a simplification of the pattern of the arable landscape due mainly to larger field sizes, resulting in a lower diversity which is important to hares'.

No matter what the reason given for the hare's decline, the fact that sports which involve the hunting of the hare in its various forms enjoy such an enthusiastic following can only bode well for the hare's future. The Waterloo Cup held each year at Altcar requires many hares in order to ensure a successful meeting and there will always be some enthusiasts in a position to ensure that sufficient hares are on the ground to enable them to carry out their chosen sport.

For a long time it has been the practice to move hares from one part of the country where they are plentiful and transport them to places with a lower density or even complete absence, with a view to including a new meet on the card one day. The ways of catching hares are easy enough and the old-time poacher knew the value of a gate-net but such methods are not really relevant to a book on beagling especially when, as it is now thought, hares moved from their home environment fail to adapt to new surroundings, and after only a few weeks well over 50 per cent of the numbers released

The poacher's traditional means of taking a hare — the gatenet. Nets could also be used to move hares from one area of the hunting country to another where they were scarce, but whether this is an effective means of distributing the potential quarry is open to question

will be unaccounted for when it comes to carrying out a hare census. Another census taken after months rather than only weeks will probably show even less in the way of any hares which might have been successfully adapted to their new environment.

This failure to survive is not surprising: when a well-intentioned moving operation is carried out the stress of being netted, bagged or boxed is often enough to cause death within minutes. Hares which do reach their chosen destination will then possibly have to try and change their feeding habits. After all, if there is no nucleus of stock already there, something must be wrong with the area and, as we have seen the most likely reasons will be to do with diet.

It has been suggested that these methods would be rather more successful if the hares were allowed to become accustomed to the area over a period of time by being kept at first in a penned area and treated in the manner of pheasant poults before being released at an appropriate time. However, reports from France (where this has already been tried) do not sound too encouraging.

The master of a beagle pack is, of course, entirely in the hands of the landowner over whose land his hounds hunt but it is reasonable to assume that no person wishes to see the total eradication of a species and even where hare shooting is carried out by the estate there should still be enough hares around to make a visit worth while. Indeed, for the purposes of providing some good hunting, a visit after one of these shoots is probably preferable to one before, when the abundance of hares is bound to lead to the pack splitting as one hare rises in front of another.

Thinking like a hare

Half the pleasure in following a pack of beagles is in attempting to anticipate the hare's movements so as to get to a good vantage point and see the whole of the hunt taking place. The inexperienced follower, provided he can run fast enough, will see them draw for their quarry and, on a good scenting day, hunt her away over the hill, but what then? Even the huntsman will probably not see the next twenty minutes or so but, in between pauses to navigate the next barbed-wire fence or gasp for breath, the follower may find time to notice that little group of septuagenarians leaning against the shelter of a tree on a windswept hill, involved in nothing more than an idle chat. However, there is no doubt that they will already have seen much more than he has, purely and simply because they know

At times the hare shows great resource and cunning. She is, however, often content to crouch at the first sign of danger, only leaping up and moving off when hounds get too close for comfort. Occasionally her decision to move comes too late with the inevitable result that hounds 'chop' her whilst still in the form; a kill to keep hounds in blood but nothing more

where the action is likely to be. These people know where the hare is likely to travel and can position themselves accordingly.

The hare is a creature of habit and its form is carefully chosen to give not only easy access to food but also to give a view, and shelter from the prevailing wind. Most of the day is spent in this form and, if alarmed the hare will at first crouch, only leaping up and moving off when hounds approach too close for comfort. A hare leaving its form takes no precautions but will run straight to its chosen exit from the field. Many experienced huntsmen feel that the hare's choice of route when first leaving its form will often determine its future movements during the rest of the hunt and it is common to hear a huntsman remark on a 'left-handed hare' and, at a check for instance, he will cast his hounds in a left-handed direction, feeling that once she has chosen her course she will stick to it, whatever the circumstances.

By moving forward cautiously and at a steady pace, the hare is able to assess what is happening both in front and behind, frequently standing on her hind legs the better to judge this. Where possible she will always run uphill and will try to return to the same field as her form, even though she has only very recently been disturbed, and apparently a hare will almost always be back on home ground within two hours of being found. When pressed hard by the hounds, the hare is capable of seeming to be every bit as cunning as a fox and gets up to every trick that a hunted fox has been known to use and quite a few which he has not. It is, however, probably only a coincidence that both species will often pass through a herd of cows or a flock of sheep when hounds are close; after all, it would be unreasonable to give an animal the kind of thinking power which enables it to work out logically that such a move will foil the scent and gain more time.

Several experienced followers of hounds claim that the hare is able to switch off its scent glands when being pursued, in the same way that a sitting gamebird masks her scent at a time when she is most vulnerable to the unwanted attentions of predators but, if this

(above) Miss Wilkinson and Charles Vivian, joint-masters of the Meon Valley, at a meet *(Geoff Burch)*
(below) Roy Clinkard, master and huntsman of the Aldershot beagles, at the 1986 opening meet *(Richard Hedger)*

were indeed the case, surely no hunt would ever experience a good hunting day?

There is no doubt that animal scent, artificial fertilisers and water will help a hare to gain several extra minutes but probably the dodge most often used to throw the hounds is that of running through a hedge so as to be out of sight and to run on into the field for about 50 yards before turning back on exactly the same line and then running back into the hedge. Along this the hare then often runs before taking several large jumps in order to leave as little scent as possible. Alternatively she sometimes, upon reaching the middle of the field, runs in a circle before once again leaping off to one side or the other.

A sight seen by too many people too many times to be merely a coincidence is that of a tired hare putting up a fresh one and then squatting in the vacated form.

Possibly because of this immense resourcefulness, whether it be reasoning or instinct, a large proportion of hares get away from the pack. It is reckoned that only one in ten is killed by hounds. Indeed, the only reason why hares are caught is because they are animals of very little stamina, whereas the beagle has considerable amounts of the same. Of course, scenting conditions need to be ideal and the hare knows much more about these conditions than do the hounds, the hunt staff or the most knowledgeable of followers; because of this, hunting is not the 'ruthless war of lung-shattering attrition' that some opponents of beagling would have us believe. It must be remembered that beagles are only one of the many enemies of the hare and certainly not the most important. Perhaps it is because of the day-to-day vigilance necessary to avoid predators that the hare can often disappear, as if by magic, when pursued by hounds.

Legend, fiction and mythology

It is this ability to disappear without trace which has led to the hare being associated with witchcraft and there is no doubt that the hare is a timid, rather mysterious creature which has long been connected with religion and superstition.

(above) A cross-section of beagling supporters *(Richard Hedger)*
(below) At a kill *(Richard Hedger)*

To primitive man the horse, lamb and hare were mediators of the sacred and it was unheard of to eat the flesh of the hare. In Ireland this feeling apparently still exists to some extent and is probably due, in part, to the fact that the hare is also supposed to be a witch in disguise. Whereas not that many years ago the country people would admit to not eating hares, today they will not admit to anything so stupid; they just do not eat hares.

In Christina Hole's *English Folklore* there is mention of the witch of Winterslow. Living during the early years of the last century, Lyddie Shears was supposed by her fellow villagers to be able to turn herself in a hare. When not thus engaged, she still managed to possess some kind of power over the local hare population and it was said that potential poachers used to give her presents if she would promise to find their quarry for them. Upon receiving the various gifts, Lyddie would travel on to the downs, where she would strike lights from a flint and hares would show themselves in every direction, allowing the poachers to kill them whilst they were still dazzled by the flashes. Such powers were not enough to save Lyddie's life, however, and the witch of Winterslow was eventually shot dead by a silver bullet whilst running as a hare and was later found dead in her cottage with the bullet in her heart.

According to legend, the doe in Noah's Ark was drowned and only the buck was left to propagate the species. Because of this, God gave the buck the ability to produce leverets alone and even as late as the seventeenth century it was thought that the male could produce offspring. Sir Thomas Browne, writing *Inquiries into Common and Vulgar Errors*, believed that the sexes were interchangeable in hares and that the buck was capable, on occasions, of giving birth to young. The people of ancient Greece held the same opinion, and the old laws of Wales, which set out the relative values of many animals (including cats) and set different prices for male and female of various ages, put no price on the hare because it was female one month and male the next. The belief probably stems from religion where the perfect body is spiritually and physically hermaphrodite or, more specifically, as Adam was before Eve was made from his body and produced a separate person (*Genesis* 2, 18–22).

Some ancient writers believed that not only are the sexes interchangeable in hares but also that the leverets were formed in separate wombs. Claudius Aelianus, writing in the third century, claimed also that the hare 'carried some of its young half formed in its womb, some it is in the process of bearing, others it has already borne'. Although such a procedure seems impossible it is now found that hares are unique in being able to conceive a second time even when already pregnant. Scientifically this is known as 'super-foetation'.

Even in these days of modern research it is obvious that some areas of the hare's habits remain something of a mystery and, in certain cases, fact intermingles with fiction.

For many years there was a theory that hares chewed the cud in the same manner that cows regurgitate all that they have eaten and chew it thoroughly before swallowing it again, but it is only recently that it has been discovered that the first time the food is eaten by hares it is only partially digested, compressed and softened. Refection, first noticed in rabbits, is a regular habit of the hare but, unlike cattle and sheep, partially digested food is passed through the body before being eaten again. The droppings which are refected differ in appearance from those which are finally discarded.

Also common to both rabbit and hare is the heavy mortality rate among the embryos which are then reabsorbed, but there any similarities end and the two species seldom occupy the same areas in any great numbers.

Old beliefs maintained that the buck rabbit would kill any young hares which it came across and Woodruffe-Peacock, in his *Cultivation of the Common Hare*, published in 1905, stated that 'when rabbits are abundant, they bully, chase and worry hares to death'. Gamekeepers have seen evidence of this carnage in the hare population but it is more likely that the real reason that hares and rabbits do not fraternise is because grass on ground on which rabbits have fed seems to be fouled for the hare.

Some facts about the hare can be neither confirmed nor denied. Who, for instance, has been able to prove the theory long held by country writers that it is only the females of the species which live in the same area all their lives, the bucks wandering into strange territories, or that it is possible to distinguish between the sexes by the way in which the animals carry their ears? (The doe is said always to carry hers laid flat, and the buck keeps one of his slightly cocked.)

No wonder, then, that the hare has such appeal. Many years ago Brockwell Ysgythrong, Prince of Powis, hunted a hare into a cave which also harboured a young damsel named Monacella, who was hiding after refusing to marry the nobleman husband of her father's choice. The prince was so touched by the sight of her cradling the trembling hare to her bosom that he founded an abbey in her name. Thereafter it was believed that if anyone cried 'God and St Monacella be with thee' when a hare was pursued by dogs, it was sure to escape!

Centuries ago, the Bilsdale hunt of North Yorkshire turned to hunting foxes after the huntsmen had one day chased a hare into the garden of an old hag thought to possess magical powers and were faced with a breathless and very angry old woman. She was probably not a witch, as they thought, but more likely the original founder of the League Against Cruel Sports!

5
THE HUNT STAFF
AND THEIR DUTIES

Ask any experienced beagler what makes a successful beagle pack and he will probably tell you that it is the huntsman. Press him further and then ask what makes a good huntsman; he will, without any hesitation, reply that it is one who is quiet and loves his hounds.

Whilst this probably oversimplifies things, there is a lot of truth in such a short answer and it is for this reason that I intend to start by describing the duties of the huntsman rather than subscribe to protocol and etiquette and accept that the master is, traditionally, of greater importance.

The huntsman

Of course without the ground, a plentiful supply of hares and well-bred hounds, no huntsman, no matter how good, can show a good day's hunting but the person who has a feel for the sport will probably be able to give the field a reasonable day when other, more mediocre huntsmen have had to take hounds home, leaving both the pack and the followers frustrated.

The best huntsman is probably one who is involved in the day-to-day running of the kennels and who, because of his involvement with feeding and exercising, knows his hounds and their individual idiosyncracies.

Ideally, then, the huntsman should be professionally employed but, in beagling circles at least, the professional huntsman is something of a rarity. Commander Forbes, writing at the turn of the century, pointed out that 'the difference between an amateur and a professional huntsman is that one swears at you, whereas, as a rule, the other does not'.

In fact there is no reason why an amateur who has natural abilities and a real liking for the job should not make as good, or even better, a huntsman than a professional, provided of course that he is prepared to devote as much time as possible to being with his hounds. He will in all probability have first become interested in hound work as a casual observer before being given the opportunity to carry a whip, during which time he will have learnt to think not only like a beagle but, more importantly, like a hare, whilst at all stages he is doing the job because he wants to rather than because he is paid to do so. His position should inspire more confidence in himself and give a sense of authority that the professional sometimes lacks, while the feeling of *noblesse oblige* will prevent his developing a certain slackness and anxiety to put in an easy day that becomes noticeable in some paid officials after a time.

I think the reason that Commander Forbes felt that the field was more likely to be damned by an amateur huntsman rather than by a professional was because if, for instance, the huntsman is interfered with by the supporters when at a cast or making a check, a professional may not point out his displeasure to them and risk losing his job, whereas the amateur has nothing of any consequence to lose. Both should, however, have a master who is renowned for his diplomacy and it is up to him to keep the field in check so that the huntsman can keep his eyes on the pack and have no need to divide his attention between his hounds and their followers.

Of course, the ideal huntsman should have a smiling face and a good word for everyone, save under the most exceptional circumstances, and it certainly gives more pleasure being out with a pack which is hunted by such a man than would be obtained by hunting with a man who is always frowning and who, on the rare occasions when he does open his mouth, will only moan about the scarcity of hares, poor scenting or the fact that 'so and so', who ought to know better, has just headed the hare. After all, beagling is merely a pastime to most of the field and all have come out to enjoy themselves. Having said this, the field does have a certain responsibility and people must remember that it is necessary for the huntsman to be close to his hounds in order to handle them. If followers are breathing down his neck, they will undoubtedly hamper him and also spoil their own sport: hounds will not, and cannot, do their best with crowds of people close to their heels.

How the huntsman deals with such a situation is often a measure of his competence. When hunting hounds with a field which is too eager, the thinking huntsman will, although he knows that it is advisable to be closer to his hounds, keep well back, knowing that if he goes forward the field will follow him and probably get the beagles' heads up.

Often, when the hounds have had a hitherto good run and have subsequently checked, the huntsman will not be near them and when he gets up, his handling of them must be, to a large extent, a matter of guesswork. He will notice many things which will materially help him to make his cast successfully but he will only act after the hounds have first made their cast. He will see exactly where they lost their line, which way they seemed inclined immediately prior to losing it, what his old and reliable hounds were doing at that moment, and whether they seem disposed to go forward or back, left or right.

A very experienced huntsman who knows his hounds well will sometimes, when they check, be able to tell from their behaviour that they think their hare is down. He must therefore know his charges and recognise their foibles and failures and whether they can be relied upon when they speak. By watching hounds he will notice that when one lifts his head, sniffs and goes from left to right, that particular beagle is deciding from just which direction the smell arises.

Great emphasis must be placed on the huntsman's ability to observe. A certain amount of his hunting procedures can be learnt from books and there is no doubt that some of the foxhunting classics written by Peter Beckford, Isaac Bell and Thomas Smith, many years ago, contain much information which is still relevant. They will only prove really useful, however, after much personal observation and practical hunting which will enable the reader to say to himself, 'Ah yes, my hounds did exactly the same last Saturday'. As with observing any form of country life it should also be remembered that, although nine hares have made an identical manoeuvre at the same time and maybe even at the same place, the tenth hare will do something totally different and so the huntsman (or anyone else, for that matter) should never fall into the trap of thinking that, because he has seen it many times, a hare or hound will *always* do that. He will be more successful if he thinks that, in such a situation, the animal *usually* or *almost always* performs in a certain way but at the same time he must be ready to cover any other eventuality.

Another point which the huntsman should always bear in mind is that different meets often require different hunting techniques. This is especially important when the master or huntsman is in the habit of organising 'away days': a week as part of the Northumberland Beagling Festival, or invitation meets or, as the end of the season approaches, perhaps a day as a guest of another pack in his old stamping-grounds. Not only is there the added pressure of impressing foreigners with the pack's prowess but failure is almost bound to arise when a huntsman tries methods which work well on grassland in some less favoured country. A 14 inch beagle will find the stone walls and rough terrain of a country which is normally hunted by heavy 16 inch hounds difficult enough without the added disadvantage of a huntsman who is not prepared, or even able, to adapt his techniques to suit the ground.

Many hunting authorities consider that the test of a good huntsman is to be found in his ability to recover the line quickly and efficiently at a check but I wonder whether a fairer test would be his ability to show good sport no matter what the terrain.

Throughout the hunt, the huntsman will have some idea as to where his hare is heading, especially when it is a meet which is visited frequently and he has the knowledge of what line previous hares have taken so that, when the hounds at last make it obvious that they can do no more, he will instantly be able to decide on the best course of action. He will not, however, rush his hounds and if he is really careful they will not be aware that they have been helped.

Whether in kennels or out on the hunting field, a good huntsman will attend to his exceptional hounds rather than cater for the majority. If they are favourably exceptional he knows that he can rely on them, and if exceptional because of appearing slightly retarded or backward his encouragement may well turn a mediocre hound into an outstanding one.

It is an interesting fact (though perhaps not a surprising one bearing in mind the above) that a hound will often give its attention to the huntsman rather than to the man who feeds it. A huntsman

Roy Clinkard and the Aldershot beagles moving off from the opening meet in 1986. A hound is often more devoted to its huntsman than to the person who feeds it. To achieve this, however, it is imperative that hounds have total confidence in their huntsman, irrespective of whether or not he is the one with the 'meal ticket'

must know his hounds well and have their confidence if they are to be reasonably obedient to his orders, despite the excitement which often occurs when a large field is present. It is confidence, and the knowledge that perseverance in the right direction will be rewarded, that provides drive — the quality that distinguishes the successful pack. He should encourage confidence by all means in his power.

The huntsman must not nag his hounds or give orders purely from the desire to hear his own voice and show followers that he is in charge. The ultimate accolade for a huntsman should be for members of the field to say, 'He hunts them well and how quiet he is with them. In fact you hardly ever hear his horn or his voice'.

It is the whippers-in who should be responsible for any discipline which may be required and after a rating from them beagles should return to their huntsman for reassurance; his job is one of encouragement, not remonstration. On the rare occasions when he does have to raise his voice, perhaps to lift hounds in order to stop them rioting, hopefully such a departure from the norm will be enough to stop them in their tracks. We all remember just how effective a reprimand from the normally easygoing teacher at school was, as opposed to the constant nagging from one of his or her colleagues!

Whatever happens on the hunting day, it is certainly desirable for the huntsman to be reasonably fit so that he can keep his hounds in sight. The spectacle of a huntsman plodding along half a mile behind the majority of the field is rather an ignominious one, especially when he is so far behind that the field is at a check before him and is not restrained from pressing too close on hounds.

The huntsman needs to be just as good a diplomat for his sport as is the master and in addition his 'man management' should be faultless. He will need to delegate responsibility both around the kennels and on the hunting day. When planning on the positioning of his whippers-in for a certain meet, he should be able to inform them of his intentions so that they can do their job efficiently and yet not leave them with the feeling that he is pushing them away from the action. As we shall see when discussing the duties of the whippers-in, they will often miss most of the fun, keeping guard along the side of a road, railway or pheasant covert, and it is up to the huntsman to impress upon them their importance in performing such a duty and yet still manage to maintain their interest. Having spent several hours on a quiet moorland road on the off-chance that a vehicle might come along, and seen nothing of the hunting because the hare chose to go in the opposite direction, I know just how important it is for the huntsman to take the time and trouble to make the whip feel that he is the most valuable person around.

Finally, it is important that the huntsman takes a pride in his personal appearance. For those who do not know the pack and who have never had the opportunity to visit the kennels, the turn-out of the huntsman and his whippers-in, and the cleanliness of hounds and hound van, is often used as a measure of how hounds are treated and the hygiene in the kennels. There is no excuse for a scruffy start to the day. The green beagling jacket can be taken to the meet on a coat-hanger and protected by a dry-cleaner's bag and the breeches can be protected whilst drawing and vanning hounds by a light pair of nylon over-trousers. Even small, inconsequential items should not be overlooked. It is an easy matter to polish up the horn but don't forget boots and even the whip-thong.

One pair of boots is not likely to be sufficient and the huntsman should possess at least two pairs so that one set can be dried and subsequently polished before being subject to the public gaze. Boots suitable for the follower are discussed in the chapter on 'The Hunting Day', but the hunt staff will choose their footwear with even greater care and, for many, Dunlop Green Flash seem to answer most requirements.

The mud which gathers on the whip handle and thong must be cleaned after each outing. Apart from anything else, great lumps of clay sticking to the handle do not make for a comfortable grip and if the thong is not carefully treated and preserved it will soon dry and crack, involving unnecessary expense in its replacement.

A final requirement for any huntsman should perhaps be a thick skin: in any group of followers there will always be several present who could hunt hounds better. The fact that criticism of the hunting is one of the worst breaches of manners, for which no excuse can be found, seems not to deter these people one little bit and the huntsman will soon hear that, in the opinions of some, he has made

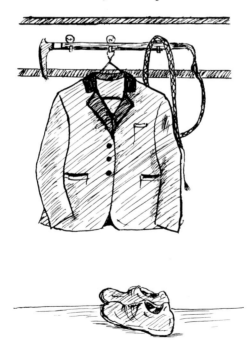

Clean jacket, clean whip and the right sort of footwear; all essential if the hunt staff is to give the right impression

the wrong cast, such and such a hound is babbling and it never has been worth while drawing this field. If something goes wrong, it is bound to be the huntsman's fault!

The masters

It is not unusual for the master of a beagle pack to hunt his own hounds or, where a joint mastership exists, for one of the masters to carry the horn. In some ways, combining the duties of huntsman and master makes the whole operation run that little bit sweeter — cutting out the middle man if you like. On the negative side, however, the work load is doubled and the points outlined above are just as applicable to the master as they are to the huntsman.

One of the first things a new master must do on assuming office is to get hold of an Ordnance Survey map of his country and a notebook. On the map, the usual and traditional meets should be marked, together with the acreages normally covered during the course of the hunt. Farms and estates can be pencilled in and the names and addresses of those who it will be necessary to see at a future date can be written in the notebook. Even if the new master is well acquainted with his country, this exercise is still well worth while and will be a source of continual reference throughout the whole of his mastership.

As the planning of the meet card and most of the hunting arrangements fall on his shoulders, he should then take the time to go out and introduce himself to those landowners who are not seen during the natural course of events such as hound exercise or flesh collection. On the master's imaginary curriculum vitae one of the first essentials must be diplomacy and if he handles himself well during these visits the hunt may be pleasantly surprised to find that the new master has managed to organise a meet on ground which had hitherto been forbidden territory. Perhaps the previous master had, for one reason or another, got on the wrong side of these people and the 'new chap' has managed to bury the hatchet through sweet talking and mentioning the fact that his brother-in-law knows a mutual friend who keeps his horse on the neighbouring ground!

It is no use laying down hard and fast rules as to how the farmers should be approached: each visit must be carried out with a particular individual in mind. It is often the ability to spot in a moment just the right attitude to adopt that makes the difference between success and failure. As David Brock observed in his book *To Hunt the Fox:*

> Some otherwise excellent sportsmen have the unhappy knack of an- tagonising every farmer they meet . . . [whereas] though he may be the worst of huntsmen, though he be not able to produce one squeak from his horn, though he may be a veritable duffer across a country, if the master is looked upon as a personal friend in every farmhouse in his country he is a success . . . Fortunate indeed is the hunt which is warned off no farm nor covert . . .

Like the huntsman, the master should be good at delegating respon- sibility and, to outward appearances at least, he should rule the hunt with the proverbial rod of iron. His decision on a hunting day especially should always be obeyed without question. Hunt ser- vants are considered to be employed by a master or joint masters who as such have authority over them. Such rules avoid any possi- bility of a disagreement as to policy in the field. In order to create the respect necessary for this from his staff (whether professional or amateur is immaterial) the master must be seen to be out hunting on a regular basis.

The master should work through the hunt secretary and the com- mittee and, although there is a vast difference between a hunt which is run by a committee and a hunt which has a committee, they should consult the master before making any major decisions, whatever the circumstances. He will in any case deal with all ad- ministrative problems, in particular making sure that all the hounds are vaccinated.

No master of hounds or hunt committee should endeavour to en- gage another hunt servant who is not known to be disengaged at the end of the current hunting season, without first liaising with the in- dividual's present master. No matter what the situation, it is up to the master of any pack to ensure that his staff, whether they be pro- fessional or amateurs acting as such, are fully aware of the rules set out in the handbook of the Association of Masters of Harriers and Beagles.

Like a hound, whose qualities cannot properly be judged until the end of its first season and preferably its second, it is not by his first or second season that anyone can judge the capabilities of a master or huntsman. Indeed, it is unlikely that consistently good sport will be shown in the season succeeding a mastership change as the newcomer has everything to learn. Likely as not, he will have his own ideas about feeding, exercise and condition which may not have been those of his predecessor and any alteration in the treatment of hounds and in their daily routine will make a difference to the hunting. Short masterships are therefore bad for beagling in general and for the individual hunt in particular. Obviously there are situations where short masterships cannot be avoided (school and university packs for example) but on the whole I think that most subscribers would prefer continuity in the interest of good sport.

A point which perhaps a potential master might bear in mind is that of forming a joint mastership for a season or two with one who intends to retire. By sharing the responsibility it is often possible to learn from him all that is to be known about the country and the best way in which to hunt it. There can be no better preparation for the beginner than for him to share the work with a practised master of hounds who has every relevant detail at his fingertips.

It used to be reckoned that, for the privilege of all his power, the master required bottomless pockets but, as a general rule, today's masters need no longer actually finance the hunt: subscription packs have done away with this. Undoubtedly they will be out of pocket, what with donations to various raffles, prizes for hunt functions, entertaining and petrol expenses, but even so mastership is not beyond the aspirations of most of us. For example, at least three masters registered with the association are milkmen who not only subscribe in the above way for the benefit of the hunt but also manage to find the time to do their milkround, help out in kennels and, during the season, hunt hounds themselves.

Nevertheless it may be useful to quote Mr Delme Radcliffe, a master of hounds in the 1830s, whose comments still apply today to a greater or lesser degree: '. . . a master of hounds would always find his hand in his pocket, and must always find a guinea there'. Had he written these words at a later date, he may have said 'both hands in both pockets'; but in a properly managed country a smaller sum than today's equivalent of the guinea should do to line the pocket of the modern master, who will find that what he gets out of the position will more than recompense him for what he puts in.

The whipper-in

Whippers-in in the beagling world are almost always amateurs, do not have the distinction of initials after their name, and very often see nothing of the day's hunting. Despite these facts it would be rare to find a hunt actually looking for a whipper-in. There is always someone ready and willing to undertake the responsibility. Some packs are, however, in my opinion, often understaffed in this department.

Whippers-in are expected to perform many duties. At the end of the day one or two tired hounds may need assistance over a sheep fence or a thick hedge. During the actual hunting most beagles can overcome almost any obstacle

How many whips are considered necessary must depend on the individual hunt and the country over which it hunts. A pack stuck out in the wilds with no roads, railways or boundaries to contend with could be hunted by the huntsman alone, but how many packs are in that fortunate position?

It must be better to see a hunt over-whipped rather than one which is understaffed. The number of places where hounds have to be stopped from going into one place or another is enormous, and the more whippers-in present, the less trouble is likely to occur. Again whippers-in are human (despite evidence to the contrary!) and they will tire if they have too much to do but, even so, they must also have the stamina of a long-distance runner, for running over plough will take it out of even the strongest person.

The list of requirements necessary to make a good whipper-in seems to be endless. Because they are out of sight for most of the hunt, they must be totally reliable and trustworthy. If a huntsman lets hounds hunt further than he ought, thinking that a whip is on the side of a road or ready to prevent hounds crossing on to forbidden ground if necessary, only to find that half the pack has been run over or that the hunt is in the centre of legal proceedings purely and simply because the relevant whipper-in was sharing a hip-flask and a cigarette with a friend, miles from where he was thought to be, that particular whip is obviously not going to be a credit to his uniform. Should a disaster occur in such a situation the hunt should take a leaf from British Rail's book and hold an inquiry. It may well turn out that the whip was in the correct place at the right time but everyone must remember that beagles travelling at 23 miles an hour take some stopping and even the most vigilant of whips can be unsuccessful. Almost as importantly, when hounds do need to be stopped, the whole operation should be carried out quickly and quietly. 'Least said, soonest mended.'

'Must know his individual hounds, use his initiative, be able to think like a hare, know his country so that he can anticipate movements of the hares/deer/hounds.' All these are suggestions put forward by masters and huntsmen when describing their ideal whipper-in and all do, in fact, play an important part in the formation of a good team.

What the whipper-in sees must always be assimilated in his brain; it might be useful at a later date. Birds rising in a field, sheep running and crowding together, or a splash in a stream, may all form an important part of a successful hunt if the whip can read the signs correctly. His knowledge will, almost by instinct, enable him to do the right thing every time, and keep his place in relation to hounds with half the effort of his less gifted brother.

Sometimes the whip will find himself the sole official of the hunt at a time when hounds are looking for help. On such an occasion no good is likely to result from awaiting the huntsman's arrival as he may still be several fields away and precious time is being wasted. In such a situation the whip's first action should be to make sure that hounds do not change on to a fresh hare. If it is felt necessary to turn them, the whip must remember to get to the far side of the hounds. It is unfortunately all too common a sight to see someone well in the midst of hounds, trying to turn them one way or another, with the effect that the pack simply scatters in all directions. The extra work involved in reaching the correct position is more than repaid by a quick result.

Nine out of ten whips interfere before they should but, on the other hand, hounds should never be left to feel that they are getting away with anything. If it is necessary to hit a hound, be sure to do so only when it is actually engaged in wrongdoing. Furthermore, be absolutely certain that, in swiping at the offender, you do not inadvertently hit another hound which is not guilty. Such action may make a delicate hound turn away from hunting and it is often those beagles which react to the tone of voice alone which, in the long run, make the best workers.

The rating of hounds is so much better than striking them with a whip. It should be done with discord in the voice. A dog does not understand the meaning of the spoken word and if you tell it that it is a 'good dog' in harsh way its tail will undoubtedly sink between its legs. Conversely, try telling it that it has been a 'right little so-and-so' in a sweet manner, and its tail will wag and there will be no stopping it from coming right up for some affection. This is logical when one remembers that encouraging notes on the horn are harmonious and those which denote rioting and so on are not. (This may be due in part to the pack instinct for it will also have been noticed by those involved that when hounds 'sing' in kennels they are always in tune.)

At the risk of dismaying many, may I suggest that the person who is commonly thought of as being the 'first whipper-in' should also carry a horn? It must, however, be made clear that he should never use it unless he is quite sure that the huntsman is not within hearing distance and that it should only be used for the purpose of collecting hounds.

When the masters and huntsman have selected the scene of the first draw, they will have already told the whips of their intentions. Indeed, having travelled in various hound vans, I know that such decisions have been made the night before. The positioning of whips will also have already been outlined, usually from previous experience, but this does not mean that the whips should rush off at the meet whilst in full view of hounds. Such behaviour will only succeed in exciting hounds and will render them wild at the start. Better to let the whips slip off quietly and as much out of sight as possible. In theory they should remain wide of the pack throughout the day but in practice the course of the hare will make this almost impossible.

If the meet is held close to the kennels, hounds may be walked to the venue. Although it is normal for the huntsman to lead his pack, with whips both flanking and behind, some masters and huntsmen prefer to follow the fashion set by some foxhunting packs half a century ago and have the first whipper-in leading. In this way, they feel, even whilst walking along the road, hounds are encouraged to be in front of their huntsman, a position which is obviously desirable in the hunting field.

At any time when they are walking with hounds as a pack, whips should remember that they must not crowd them and must allow individuals to empty themselves.

If the road is very twisty and there is likely to be a certain amount of traffic, it is often a good idea to send one of the whippers-in a hundred yards in front of the pack so that he can warn drivers to slow down. I was once present at a hunt where this was being done and a particular driver refused to slow down. With great presence of mind, the whipper-in concerned held his whip by the thong and threw the rest, handle first, straight into the windscreen of the car — a drastic move but nevertheless effective. Although the police were ultimately involved, they were found to be on the side of the hunt.

Apart from a situation similar to the above, the whippers-in should never be seen together as this obviously means that some part of the country is being left unattended. In their correct position they will be able to help the huntsman by holding up a hat or handker-

Some whippers-in tend to be rather over-officious in carrying out their duties. Sensible whips will give the pack a chance to empty themselves and settle down before beginning the day

chief at the moment when the pack is obviously in difficulty. It may be that the huntsman thinks that hounds are on the hunted hare whereas, because of his placing, the whip sees that hounds have changed hares in an undulation in the ground which made the transfer impossible for the huntsman to see. Then perhaps this is one of the rare times that the whip can holloa in order to attract the attention of both the huntsman and the hounds. A reliable whip will have the attention of the huntsman straightaway. Having holloaed, the whip should leave things alone; if the huntsman has not heard his shout, then a further hundred holloas will not be heard, and if he has heard but still refuses to react, the whipper-in can be certain that there is a very good reason.

If it looks as though the huntsman has heard and is ultimately going to bring hounds up, the whip can use his time profitably by holding up any odd beagles which may have owned the true line. As a general rule, less than four couple should be stopped; the presence of more than that number usually implies that the pack is hunting the line out and these are momentarily the leading hounds. In this case, the whip should allow them to continue but he must keep in touch with them until the huntsman and the rest of the pack have caught up with him and the whole situation can be explained.

The turning of hounds from a covert or forbidden ground has already been explained but the possibility of a whipper-in turning the hare has not yet been discussed.

The pack for which I had the pleasure to whip-in would have taken a very dim view of anyone turning a hare and, in my opinion, quite rightly. The whole point of beagling is to pit the hare's knowledge of her ground against the nose of a hound. In theory, the hare should have the upper hand, knowing her territory well. Everyone knows how easy it is to catch a rabbit which has been captured, bagged and then released on strange ground. A hare which has been turned from her intended course is, potentially, as easy a target, but many members of hunt staff can see nothing wrong with turning a hare if it means that the hunt can continue and I must admit that it cannot do a pack any good whatsoever if they are continually being whipped off their legitimate quarry. Therefore, where it is felt necessary to turn a hare, once again the whips must act quickly and quietly.

The whippers-in must also have a flair for all things canine. The difference between a man 'in tune' with dogs and one who will never possess a good dog all the time that he has a brain in his head is nowhere more easily demonstrated than on the shooting field. On the one hand a certain keeper or shooter will be able to produce a string of gundogs which will be the envy of all who see them, whilst on the other, no matter how many hundreds of pounds a gun has paid for a labrador or spaniel from the right stock, within a few weeks of taking on the animal it will be no better than a lurcher or 'long dog', running in, chasing birds and crunching those which it retrieves.

Whippers-in can be divided into the same types. One may be immaculate in his uniform, utterly charming amongst a group of subscribers and a prominent member of the committee, organising events and squeezing the last penny from even the 'tightest' of supporters. He has his place but, in the opinion of many, is not worth half as much as the person who understands dogs in general and hounds in particular. Newly entered hounds will benefit from the attentions of the latter type of whip as particular care needs to be exercised during the early part of the season. Like the huntsman, he should not nag at hounds unnecessarily, for they will resent such treatment, and he must avoid rating them and telling them to 'ware' this and that and the other, just for the sake of doing so. Owners of gundogs are apt to get into the habit of doing this, not because they want them to obey but just to satisfy themselves and any onlookers that they are the boss and the dogs merely servants. Similarly, to nag them and then be distracted, not ensuring that the dog or hound has done as it has been asked, will only result in a half-hearted response and eventually no response at all. Obedience is essential but once it has been taught there is no need to practise it unnecessarily.

Isaac Bell, in his contribution to the *Foxhunting* (1936) volume of the Lonsdale Library series, points out:

> The crack of a whip should be a signal to a hound to desist from what he is doing, and should correspond to the word 'back'.
>
> Therefore it is a mistake if you wish your hounds to hold it as such, to crack your whip while drawing a covert or for a whipper-in to crack his whip in putting hounds on to their huntsman.
>
> A whipper-in should encourage a hound on to his huntsman or on to the cry in a cheery voice.
>
> It is of little use rating a hound for a certain misdemeanour, and then hoping to reach him with a whip. As soon as it is rated it will tuck in its stern and rush to the huntsman, and then bury itself into the middle of the pack and stay there until the end of the day, keeping well out of the way of the whipper-in. If it is necessary to punish a hound, it should therefore be hit first, and then rated.

6

LIFE IN THE KENNELS

Kennel construction

Kennels are the premises on which hounds are kept; lodges and lodge yards are the buildings in which the beagles sleep and spend most of their day.

There cannot be any hard and fast rules about the layout or management of kennels, for so much depends on what is available, the pack's individual requirements and prevailing conditions.

The position and the materials of which kennels are built are of paramount importance but it is unlikely that many hunts will be in a position to do much more than update and improve an existing site as and when its finances allow. For those in the fortunate position of being able to start from scratch, however, there are many points to consider.

In order to allow for sufficient fall in the drainage, the buildings should be constructed on the highest point, with the lodges themselves facing south-east or south-south-east. Sun is of primary importance, especially in the morning when most of the lodge rooms and yards are washed down and the sun is needed to dry them as quickly as possible if one is to avoid hounds sitting in damp conditions for the majority of the day.

The sleeping quarters should not be constructed of any material which absorbs moisture or is naturally damp unless it is possible to clad the interiors completely with some form of damp-proof material. Wood is the easy answer but it has the great disadvantage of harbouring parasites. Instead, all inside surfaces must be smooth and scrubbable. The ideal would be to face the walls from floor to ceiling with ceramic tiling but, from a practical point of view, the costs involved would make the scheme prohibitive. Walls which have been faced with good quality cement and then treated with a silicone sealant which can be washed over regularly and disinfected with a preparation such as 'Formula H' provide a much cheaper and almost equally effective alternative.

Benches will also need to be considered carefully for the same reasons and, once again, although wood is the natural answer, unless the benches are portable with plenty of drainage holes bored through so that they can be taken out into the sun to be washed and aired, wood should be avoided in favour of concrete.

It might be supposed that a construction of this nature offers little in the way of warmth and comfort but when the benches are made after the manner of those in the foxhound kennels at Badminton, where the concrete has a wide pipe running right through the core of the block, they are apparently every bit as warm as beds made from wood. As the hounds lie together, their body warmth heats up the concrete and the pipe then conducts the warmth the full length of the bench.

Until quite recently it was felt that hounds did not like a high ceiling to their quarters and that they would be happier and more comfortable in buildings with a low roof. Apart from the discomfort to those whose job it is to keep the lodges clean, it is now known that

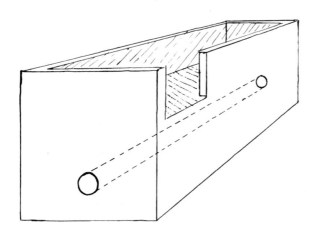

A lodge bed made of concrete with a pipe running through its centre in order to transmit heat to each individual hound using the bed

127

the higher the ceiling the better the ventilation and air flow. A low roof cuts out ventilation.

This is not to say that hounds thrive in a draughty corridor of a place. In fact a draught is any kennel dog's worst enemy and the benches must be situated in such a way as to prevent direct draughts from exits and windows.

As to the number of lodges to be built, this will depend upon the size of the pack but there will usually be at least two sleeping lodges, one for dogs and one for bitches. If a third can be accommodated, so much the better: it will prove useful as a draw yard on the hunting morning and also as a convenient place to look over a particular hound. There is also at least one other advantage in having a third lodge and this relates once again to cleanliness and hygiene. Every so often the kennel routine should include complete fumigation and this is only possible when one part of the pack can be moved to alternative quarters. Probably the best form of fumigation is still formalin, either as a liquid wash or added to potassium permanganate crystals in order to create a gaseous fume.

Each living house will have a run attached and the floor should slope from the back of the lodges and continue on a slight gradient through the yards. Sloped in this way, it is possible to wash out both lodge and yard without difficulty.

There is little point in having excessively large kennel runs. Young puppies would certainly gallop about and play in them but as they grow up they will sit about and wait to be taken out for exercise. Consequently, all that is really necessary is a run of sufficient

A lodgehouse showing the slope necessary to facilitate easy cleaning

size which will allow each and every hound a moderate amount of leg stretching and plenty of fresh air. Benches are essential in the runs and they should be low enough to the ground to prevent hounds from creeping underneath them. Where possible the run should be situated so as to allow shading from any nearby trees or so that, in an exceptionally hot summer, some form of canopy can be rigged up over it.

Traditionally, the walls and sides of the yards were constructed of brick to a height of about 3 feet, surmounted by iron bars. Today such railings would probably have to be made up specially by a blacksmith and the cost for several yards would be astronomical. Breezeblock walls, into which 12 gauge netting which also has steel bars to reinforce it every 9 inches can be cemented, is usually adequate, as is chainlink, but I have known a whippet to chew completely through the latter in a day. The doors and gates should be large enough to permit the passage of a wheelbarrow.

Anyone who has not had much experience of dogs of any breed may not, perhaps, realise what escapologists they can be. Many dogs will quite easily leap a 5 foot fence and beagles are notorious in being able to climb fences which are even higher. If this becomes a problem it may be necessary to wire in over the tops of the runs or at least have the wire turned in at the top so that a hound cannot get out over the top even if it climbs up.

Water troughs will be situated in the yards and they should be high enough from the ground to prevent hounds from soiling them. The best types are fitted with plugs for cleaning and emptying and, again from a hygiene point of view, the most satisfactory type is made from the same ceramic materials as lavatory basins and the like.

Without exception the concrete yards will lead to one or two rather larger grass runs or paddocks. On the days when exercise is not possible or hunting has finished hounds can be turned into these enclosures for a fair proportion of the day. One point which the hunt staff should bear in mind, however, is that hounds in a grass run should never be left entirely unattended in case a hound finds something of interest and a fight ensues.

Once again, chainlink fencing of 12 or 14 gauge and 2 inch mesh is ideal for the construction of these large open-topped runs. The corner posts should be well braced and the whole supported every few feet by strong stakes or, preferably, steel angle iron. The wire should be turned in and not only along the top of the fence but also

Large grass runs are useful when exercise is not possible, but the fence must be made of stout chain link held up by strong concrete posts

at the bottom in order to prevent hounds from digging out. Better still, dig a trench, bury 3 or 4 inches of wire and fill in the trench with concrete, thus cementing the wire to the ground and providing a barrier beyond which the hounds cannot burrow. It is not a bad idea, where finances allow, to widen the amount of concrete to a width of about a yard, starting with a strip across the gateway and running all the way around the inside of the paddock. This will prevent the ground from becoming a quagmire in wet, wintry weather where the hounds constantly parade up and down along the netting.

Two or more runs used in turn, so that one can be rested every few weeks and the grass given a chance to recover, would be an ideal feature of the newly constructed hunt kennel and would also cut down on the risk of worms and disease which are bound to increase with continuous use. There are many proprietary brands of disinfectant which claim to kill or at least break down disease problems associated with animals and birds kept on grass but, in the opinion of most veterinary surgeons, they are basically a waste of time, money and effort.

There is more to the layout of kennels than merely providing a home for the hounds. Close to the main lodges are usually found a cook house and store, flesh house (normally refrigerated in this day and age), draw yards and puppy show ring. For obvious reasons bitches in season will be kennelled slightly away from the majority of the pack, as will the whelping bitches. Indeed the same quarters may serve for either purpose.

Methods of feeding

Whether the cook house still retains a boiler or whether the flesh house contains much flesh is usually up to the person in charge of each particular pack. On the point of feeding, there is nothing which I or anyone else can say which will influence any future feeding programme so I do not intend to delve too deeply into the subject except to show the interested bystander a few possibilities.

Some packs feed a high proportion of cereals which are added to cooked meat and then allowed to go cold, forming a kind of pudding or porridge which can then be fed to the hounds over the next couple of days. Cooking meat will destroy vitamin B and, as this is the most important vitamin of all, a deficiency of which will lead to certain nervous disorders, brewer's yeast or 'stress' is usually added after cooking has taken place. Feeding troughs are placed in a compartment of their own (perhaps the third lodge yard?) and the hounds are allowed in. Slow-feeding hounds are usually called out by name before the rest of the pack is allowed access. Hunts which are kennelled in dairy or sheep country often get the opportunity to feed hounds on flesh casualties and although by nature dogs would probably live entirely on raw meat there are those people, including some highly respected vets, who feel that such a diet will result in bone problems and that bone meal should be added or, once a week, a feed consisting of pure wheatmeal biscuit should be included.

Methods of feeding flesh vary from pack to pack and some kennelmen will cut the flesh into small pieces whilst others merely drag a carcass into the flesh house and let the dog hounds eat one side and the bitches the other. Those who do feed raw flesh obviously do it with the hounds' best interests at heart and feel that it prevents

Feeding hounds on raw flesh

problems such as eczema, hysteria and teething fits.

On one day each week, the adult hounds are often fasted on water only, a practice carried out with carnivorous animals in most zoos as it has been found necessary to rest and cleanse the internal organs and this method seems to be the most effective.

The complete all-in-one foods which have become so popular in the gundog world in recent years could, if they were not so expensive, provide a healthy alternative to some of the more old-fashioned and well-tried ideas but the fact that one bag costing anywhere between £10 and £15 will only feed twenty-five couple of hounds once prohibits its widespread use, although a few bags kept in the stores for emergencies is probably not a bad idea.

To return to the kennel layout and the accommodation of the 'hot' and brood bitches. Once again the kennelman's idea of how to treat his whelping hounds may differ greatly from those of his neighbour a few miles up the road. In some cases it will be found that the whelping boxes will have access to concrete and grass runs; in others they will not be provided with either and, as soon as possible after giving birth, the bitch will be moved with her family into wooden kennels or hutches positioned in a grass run kept specially for the purpose.

We have already seen that whatever kennel is to be used for the accommodation of the bitches in season, it should be situated as far as is practicable from the dog hounds' kennel, and downwind of it. On no account should the drainage from there pass through the main body of lodges.

It was the fashion, some fifty years ago, to include a footbath at some point where hounds had to travel daily but it is doubtful whether walking through disinfectant once a day will do any good at all. In fact, if the bath were not properly maintained and the solution changed regularly, it could, in itself, become a breeding ground for just the type of problems it was designed to avoid. If one is provided, to do any good at all it must be long enough to prevent hounds trying to jump over it rather than going through it.

Although the footbath has been dismissed in one short paragraph, there is certainly some point in including some form of overall bath so that (especially during the summer months) hounds can be plunged into a parasiticidal shampoo in order to rid them of fleas and so on. Probably the best shampoo for this purpose would be Gamma BHC.

Where so many kennels fail is in the provision of a specifically designed sick bay and isolation ward. A surgery area equipped with a table will be helpful to the vet so that during his periodic visits he can inspect hounds at a convenient height and away from the distractions normally found near the lodges. The isolation ward will prove very useful, not only when a particular hound seems to be under the weather but also as temporary quarantine quarters for draft hounds brought in from other packs. Because of the risk of disease, they should ideally be kennelled in these quarters for at least two weeks. Hounds in general are probably more vulnerable to disease than would be the average household pet as they do not come into regular contact with dogs from outside the kennel environment and so do not get the opportunity to develop any build-up of immunity. Conversely, however, except in a situation such as outlined above, because hounds are isolated they are not as likely to pick up disease.

Warmth and cleanliness are probably the two most important factors for a successful sick bay. Clean bales of wheat straw form the best bedding, as the straw is easily swept away and burnt.

When straw is used as bedding throughout the kennels there should be a proper straw barn in which to store it. There is no point in buying good-quality straw in the autumn and then allowing it to deteriorate during the winter months purely and simply because of bad management and inadeqate covering. Under no circumstances, and no matter how short the supply of wheat straw, should the hunt be tempted to buy in barley straw. The little whiskers characteristic of this variety could do irreparable damage to the hound if they happen to find their way into the inner ear.

The premises should ideally contain a home for the huntsman or kennelman where one exists, together with a garage for the hound van and probably a few further outbuildings for general storage. Like cupboard space in an ordinary household, there are never enough places to keep those vital bits and pieces which may come in useful one day. But, to return to the problems of accommodation for any hunt staff, probably less than a third of this country's beagles are hunted by professionals and so there is not much opportunity for a hunt to offer a tied cottage as an incentive for someone to take on the job. Where a house exists as a result of more affluent times when the kennels were first built, perhaps a part-time kennelman following his own vocation will live there, his duties paying his rent. Although obviously it is better to have someone around for most of the time, thus lessening the risks (sometimes fatal) of fighting amongst hounds and also perhaps preventing the unwanted attentions of the various anti-fieldsports groups, it is not absolutely essential and several of the country's smaller packs run very successful hunts from the corner of a farmyard with a couple of visits a day made by an interested party living some miles away.

Lucky indeed are those hunts whose kennels were built by people far-sighted enough to imagine the future needs of their successors but, for the majority, the hunt must cut its coat according to its cloth.

I am tempted to use another cliché, that of cleanliness being next to godliness, for cleanliness is the first essential for any type of livestock but especially for a hound whose working ability depends on its nose. If it is continually being abused by unnecessary stench, there is no way the animal can do its job properly and not only will the hound suffer but so will the reputation of the pack.

The ease with which the kennels can be kept clean will depend

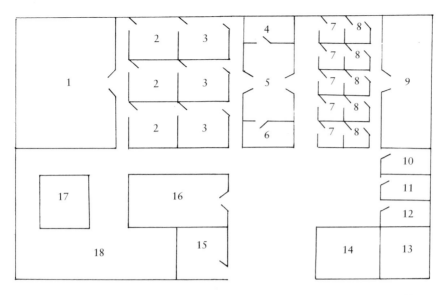

Perhaps the ideal kennel layout containing all the facilities likely to be required by a modern pack of beagles. The cost of such a purpose-built construction would, however, be prohibitive if it were built from scratch today (not to scale)

1   Main grass run
2   Lodge yards (concrete)
3   Lodges
4   Storeroom
5   Fleshhouse
6   Coldstore
7   Lodges for in-whelp or in-season bitches
8   Concrete yards for in-whelp or in season bitches
9   Grass run for in-whelp or in-season bitches
10   Bone and offal house
11   Storeroom
12   Garage
13   Garden to huntsman's/kennelman's house
14   Staff cottage
15   Isolation ward (set as close to the premises' entrance as possible so as to cut down any risk of disease from 'foreign' hounds)
16   Straw barn
17   Show ring (training and puppy shows)
18   Grassed area, maintained as a garden for the use of spectators during shows and other social events, to keep the public away from the main block of lodges. Hounds on show can, however, be brought through the concrete lodge yards and down the passage-way.

The straw barn could also be used for social events during certain periods of the year. Note also that the entrance and the reception yard are large enough to accommodate visiting vehicles plus any large lorries necessary to replenish stores and straw and collect skins, bones or offal very largely upon their construction. If the yards slope correctly towards a drain and if, in turn, the drains are never blocked and flags or concrete joinings are kept well pointed, then hygiene will be made a great deal easier.

Having looked at the construction of the buildings themselves, what of the work which goes on within their walls?

Kennel life in the summer

Kennel life during the summer months is obviously very different from that of the winter when everything has to fit around the hunting days and, as there are likely to be many more social activities going on during the warmer days, it is important to maintain the looks of the kennels.

Painting, odd-jobbing and general spring cleaning are normally carried out before the first event of the year, which is usually the puppy show. Clean kennels suggest a clean huntsman and healthy hounds and although flower beds crammed with colour and grass tracks and lawns carefully mown twice weekly will not actually produce a healthier beagle or a better hunting day, they will, without any shadow of doubt, create a good impression to the outsider who is perhaps visiting the kennels for the first time.

There are several parts of kennel routine which do not alter much in summer or winter. There will always be the chore of flesh collection for instance. Although this tends to slacken off a little during the summer as farmers finish lambing and the ills of winter disappear, it should be looked on by those responsible as a means of liaising with and offering a service in gratitude to those farmers and landowners who allow the beagles over their land.

No master should accept flesh from outside his own country without first making sure that his neighbouring masters have no objection to him doing so. This is especially important during the summer months when, for the reasons already outlined, there might not be enough flesh to go round and if one pack 'steals' from the other future relations are bound to suffer.

It is usual to collect the carcasses in the hound van and some of the more efficient packs have had the foresight to have some kind of winch attached which saves much tugging and pulling. Even a sickly sheep is heavy when it has to be lifted to 3 feet or more in order to negotiate a tailgate.

A sickly sheep is heavy when it has to be negotiated over a tailgate. Perhaps a winch attached to the hound van would avoid such problems when manoeuvring a full grown bovine casualty?

Whoever collects a carcass must make sure of just how the animal died and that by feeding it to hounds it will not put them at risk. He must also make every effort to collect flesh as soon as the farmer has notified the hunt. If he doesn't, the farmer will soon make other arrangements for its collection and, again relationships are threatened.

Whilst on the question of risk, diseases may arise from too casual an approach to the final disposal of any flesh and offal left hanging around the kennels. Skins and fleeces are usually worth a pound or two to the hunt or may be the perks of the kennelman. Either way, because there is money involved, they are not usually left too long before being collected for curing. The flesh itself is obviously accounted for, as are the paunches which, when split open and washed, form a very acceptable form of food. There is then the problem of what to do with the remainder of offal and the bones. Sometimes these are taken away for glue and cosmetics but otherwise an adequate way of disposing of them must be found on the kennel site. Burying is far from satisfactory as the quantity which has to be buried will sooner or later lead to permeation through the ground within a considerable distance of the burial place. Throwing the waste on to the dungheap is also not much good, for the same reasons, and so probably the only real alternative is to use some form of incinerator or destructor. Ideally, this should also be used for destroying soiled straw and anything else likely to put the health of either hounds or humans at risk.

Summer exercise

Although not hunting, it is still important to keep hounds reasonably fit throughout the summer but great care should be taken to ensure that they are not so fit as to make them on edge and more inclined to squabble as a consequence.

The form which exercise takes varies from kennel to kennel but all agree on the importance of the grass runs which provide a vital means of daily exercise. Some packs are more fortunate than others in that a resident kennelman who is in tune with his hounds and therefore has complete control over them can take out the kennel's full quota without the fear of them running riot on a rabbit or deer. The grass run also means that hounds can be let out from the lodges at first light whilst the sleeping quarters are being cleaned out and it is quite likely that hunts which follow this regime will then prepare the feed, letting hounds into the feed house from the runs and then returning them to the lodges. A practice carried out by many gundog kennels, and one which may be worth mentioning here, is the fact that the trainers often feed their dogs before exercise because to do things this way round leads to cleaner kennels, especially if feeding is carried out around midday. There is no doubt that a dog's first reaction after feeding is to evacuate itself and if this is done whilst out on exercise it must certainly cut down on clearing up in the kennel.

Traditions die hard, however, and it is more usual for a pack of hounds to be taken out, if not daily, at least four times a week for a period of two or three hours. Where time and personnel allow, hounds will fare that little bit better for one hour's walk each day at a steady 4 miles an hour. Being of an inquisitive nature, beagles will cover more miles during the course of the walk than will the huntsman or kennelman, especially if the walk is broken up halfway round with a stop at a suitable place in order to allow them to

It is important that the place where hounds are allowed to sniff around on exercise is chosen carefully to eliminate any risk of rioting

sniff around for a few minutes. The point should be carefully chosen to eliminate any risk of rioting. Hounds should be taught to come instantly when they are called back and probably the most effective way of ensuring strict obedience is to carry a pocketful of biscuit. After a very short while hounds will learn all about this and will fall over each other in order to return to the huntsman's pockets. 'Cupboard love', maybe, but it certainly works and once they have learnt to return they will do so irrespective of any reward received.

The exercise need not be taken in one lump, of course, and a bolt of lightning will not flash down through the skies from the fingers of the goddess Diana if these rules are not strictly adhered to! Twice daily for half an hour has the same effect. However, no matter what the time allocated, the huntsman or kennelman should try to make hound exercise as beneficial as possible to the minds of his hounds, as well as to their bodies, for it is an important time in the training of his young hounds who have joined the pack for the first time.

Now, during the summer months, is the time to teach them to swim and how to conduct themselves on the road, as well as teaching them to remain still when left unattended — a practice which, once learnt, will be useful on a countless number of occasions. It is best achieved by enlisting the help of a few keen followers. First of all, get the hounds tightly grouped; then, after giving them an appropriate command, make them stand on their own. Any attempts to follow the huntsman must be checked by his helpers. Thereafter the helpers should all move away slowly but be ready to slip back with a word of warning at the very first sign of movement on the part of any individual hound. The moment one hound is allowed to fidget or move about unchecked the rest will get out of hand but, correctly managed, the pack will soon learn.

Opportunities for further training will present themselves during hound exercise. After first of all getting the permission of the farmer, hounds can be taken right through the middle of a farmyard and given the chance to meet at close quarters sheep, young cattle, poultry and farm dogs.

When taking young hounds amongst these creatures, the huntsman should firmly forbid them to take anything other than a cursory interest in their surroundings. Anything more than this and they must be punished but only when the huntsman is absolutely certain that his hounds know, without any shadow of a doubt, that they have committed an offence.

As the summer progresses, some more strenuous exercise will be required before hunting commences and usually this is achieved by a month's hard road work, carried out daily and, for the ease of the hunt staff, on bicycles. The speed attained will be about 6 miles an hour and the effect will be to strengthen the hounds' muscles, improve their figures and harden the pads of their feet. Several masters

Summer exercise. As the season approaches, some strenuous activity will be required and, for the ease of hunt staff, this is normally carried out on bicycles

carry out a programme of exercise which owes its origins to some of the larger foxhound packs who tend to start their walking out earlier, making the initial exercise less severe. There is first of all six weeks of complete rest, followed by six weeks' gentle exercise on the road before finishing with a fortnight's really hard work. Those who subscribe to this system feel that it entails less wear and tear on their hounds than if they were allowed to get really 'soft' and out of condition and then have to undergo a sudden period of very intensive and strenuous training.

By this time any hounds which it has been found necessary to draft will have gone to their new homes and those older hounds which proved a disappointment during the last season's hunting will have been moved on or destroyed (after all, no one will thank you for passing on a hound which will not hunt). The summer months are also a good time to take a critical look at puppies of the various stages and to draft those which are not likely to conform with the standards of the hunt. Those which do can be added to the pack as they return from being out at walk and will begin to get a grasp of kennel life. How they are entered will be dealt with in a later chapter but it will be some time before they are trustworthy enough to be taken to any hound shows or allowed to parade at local agricultural events or country fairs, activities which to a lesser or greater degree form a vital part of kennel life during the summer.

Showing hounds

Not only do such shows and parades give the subscribers and members of the field the chance to meet up again and keep in touch during the break in hunting, but also such events give members of the public an opportunity to see hounds at close quarters and it is a very popular spectacle. It is best not to make the plans for a parade too ambitious. A walk around the main ring and then perhaps a trot with a quick blow on the hunting horn, and then the obligatory invitation to the children in the crowd to come into the centre of the ring and make friends with the beagles is all that is required, or indeed expected. Lucky will be the huntsman who manages to carry out even this relatively simple act of control without losing at least a couple of hounds which slip off unnoticed through the ropes.

Hound shows themselves are a more serious matter and necessitate quite a few hours of hard work on the flags at the kennels if one is to be successful. The preparation usually falls upon the shoulders

A modern-day foxhound-type of beagle, standing up in the show position 'on its toes, stern up and neck outstretched'

of the huntsman and the hounds are his responsibility when they are taken to the shows. That the huntsman needs to be skilful when showing his hounds will be obvious to the onlooker on his first visit to a show and a man who understands his charges and has their trust can persuade a bad hound to show its best points. For the best results, however, the huntsman needs to enlist the help of at least one of the whippers-in right from the start and, once again, a piece of biscuit will attract the beagles' attention prior to some intensive training.

A good plan which has been successfully used by many huntsmen is to start with two pups, collared and leashed, and then to offer them the biscuit, holding it high so that they will look upwards. In a very short space of time it will be noticed that the puppies begin to stand on their toes with sterns up and necks outstretched, already in the best position for judging.

Sometimes the incentive offered by the biscuit is not enough and a young hound which is very shy may need a little careful handling before he feels confident enough to show himself. Such cases can often be dealt with by adopting the following procedure which, I am assured, never fails, even where general kindness and petting has met with no response.

First of all, stand over the hound with a foot on either side of him and then hold your hands with the fingers spread out so that they surround the base of his neck. Then, draw the hands upwards along the neck and head to the tip of the muzzle. Do this lightly but at the same time using a fairly rapid movement. The whole operation should then be repeated several times after which, in theory at least, it should be possible to do anything with one's pupil.

The whipper-in who holds the leads also plays an important part in the show-ring as well as during training and an experienced whip seems to be completely at one with his huntsman the whole time. In some ways it is a little like the trout fisherman playing a bigger fish than his leader was designed to hold and by giving a little on the leash he will restrain the hound but, at the same time, will not prevent it from showing itself. Compare this with the antics of the inexperienced whipper-in who holds his hounds so tightly that they almost fall to the ground in their efforts to do their huntsman's bidding, legs spread out, feet scrambling and half choked. No wonder that the judges hardly spare such a team a second glance and that the huntsman's sleeve remains uncluttered by those elusive rosettes.

Health, hygiene and diseases

I make no apologies to publisher, editor or reader for returning so frequently to the question of health and hygiene in the hunt kennels. To my mind, it is the most important subject when many animals of whatever species are kept in large numbers and are continually using the same ground.

Advances in the veterinary field over the last twenty years or so have been most impressive. Improved drugs (particularly antibiotics and vaccines, as well as surgery techniques) have made life much easier for dog owners in general and hunt kennels in particular. Thanks to the combined injections against distemper, hepatitis, jaundice and parvo virus, these diseases no longer pose the threat that they once did. The isolation ward used by responsible kennelmen for any new hounds brought into the kennels means that they are able to deal with any trouble immediately it becomes evident. Distemper, for instance, may be in the incubation stages when a dog comes into the kennels and to put it straightaway with the main pack and therefore in contact with all the others might start an outbreak which could not be controlled. Any suspicious symptoms which develop can be noted promptly in the isolation ward and the hound's temperature can be taken before calling in the services of the veterinary surgeon.

The hunt should make a point of getting to know their chosen vet. It need not be the first local surgery that one notices in the Yellow Pages: the kennelman or huntsman should find a veterinary practice which shows an obvious interest in the kennels and the animals kept therein. In return, as soon as the vet sees that the kennelman really cares, he will do his best for him and no problem will be too much trouble.

Injection times can be used to let the vet see each hound for a thorough check-up, especially with regard to teeth, eyes and ears. Likely sources of infection are to be found at this stage and he will examine the eyelids for thorns, the lower lids for dust and weed seed. Cataracts and warts may also be noticed and in cases where they are likely to impede the eyesight they need to be surgically removed. Ideally, regular booster injections will be given annually; even though it is likely to cost several hundred pounds to carry out the work, it is well worth it for peace of mind. Most vets generally give a reduction when injecting three or more dogs and the hunt

Worming a hound with one of
the veterinary prescribed broad
spectrum wormers

may be able to negotiate a really good reduction for injecting a
whole pack.

Worming is extremely important and it can be carried out by
members of the hunt staff. They should use a broad spectrum
wormer, available only from their vet, and should not be tempted
into buying an 'over the counter' preparation which is generally not
so effective. Transmission of these internal parasites is facilitated
by the aggregation of large numbers of dogs sharing grass exercise
runs and so every effort should be made to clear the runs of excre-
ment regularly.

Hookworm is particularly common in hunt kennels but hardly
ever found in pet animals or show dogs. It is interesting that foxes
may act as reservoirs of infection, since the rate of the worm found
during experiments has been as high as 91 per cent in some areas.
An infection of only one thousand larvae has been found to be
enough to give a hound diarrhoea and smaller infestations are
associated with a leakage of protein into the gut which then shows
in the hound by means of digestive disorders and a generally poor

condition. In severe cases, it may show itself further with lesions on the skin and feet where the paw becomes swollen and deformities of the pads and claws can develop.

Infective larvae can develop anywhere where there is sufficient warmth and moisture. The development of the egg is influenced by weather conditions, and accounts for the fluctuation in the number of worm cases seen as the overwintering larvae die away in the spring or early summer to be replaced by a new generation, with peak numbers occuring in high summer.

Sometimes it may be noticed that certain hounds are losing condition and alternate between diarrhoea and dark evil-smelling faeces. To the lay person a definite diagnosis may be difficult but if brown, barrel-shaped eggs are noticed it is likely that the hound is a host to whipworm. The egg is very long lived and once a grass paddock is contaminated it will remain a potential source of infection for at least five years. Desiccation will kill the ova but as drought conditions occur only infrequently in Britain the only really feasible means of reducing the risk of infection is to dig and re-seed.

Two more common helminths known by all dog owners are the tapeworm and the roundworm, both of which are parasites of the bowel but which, in kennels maintaining a good standard of indoor hygiene and a regular worming programme, should not cause any serious problem. Tapeworm especially is more readily found when uncooked meat is the main source of dietary income and the flesh of both sheep and horse have been found to contain more than their fair share of tapeworm-inducing ingredients. In one survey, eleven out of twenty-one packs were affected.

Ringworm is often a problem in a kennel and because of this, as a matter of course, children should not be encouraged to play around the kennels or be unduly affectionate with the hounds.

The question of worms affecting humans should never be underestimated. Hookworm, for instance, is serious enough to the hound but is possibly more dangerous to *Homo sapiens*. As might be expected, the ova of any species are more abundant in large kennel establishments and people working in such environments would seem to be at greater risk. Man becomes infected by ingesting the sticky, embryonated eggs found in faeces or dust which have contaminated his fingers or food. When man ingests the embryonated ova of any form of toxocara, hatching inevitably takes place and the larvae will invade the tissues of the body. Although man does not function very efficiently from the parasite's viewpoint as most of the intermediate forms in human tissue are sterile and incapable of infection, hookworm, however, differs. It will affect the lungs and liver plus, in certain circumstances, the spleen, kidneys and bone marrow, leaving a hydatid cyst for which at present the only feasible remedy is surgical removal. Tapeworms also use man as an intermediate host and the result of such activity may show as one of these cysts.

Why children are more inclined to suffer from hound-induced diseases is not really known but the probable reason is that one cannot demand or expect a consistently high standard of hygiene in this age group.

Lungworm is often first noticed by coughing and may be dismissed by certain authorities as being 'kennel cough' but in actual fact, from the veterinary point of view, 'kennel cough' is a name which may have several different causes, one of which may be due to worms found in the trachea and bronchi, particularly where the two join together. Many cases are without symptoms but infection is sometimes characterised by a chronic dry cough, exacerbated by exercise, which sometimes ends with a retching action. The disease is most often seen in young hounds of around four to six months of age but can also occur in young adults. It seems likely that the larvae are transferred by an adult bitch, which is not noticeably affected, licking her offspring. Although all breeds seem equally susceptible, the parasite is particularly prevalent in hounds, with approximately one in five carrying infection.

More common forms of injury in the hunt kennels are likely to arise from wounds and, in spite of the fact that a beagle cannot, by any stretch of the imagination, be called a clean feeder, it is amazing just how quickly the most serious cuts and wounds will heal if treated in a methodical and sensible way. The whole secret is to keep them spotlessly clean, and on no account should one let them heal until they are completely clean. The cleanliness must start with the kennelman's own hands and the instruments which he uses and he must not be surprised if a hitherto clean wound becomes septic if he injects with a syringe which he has already used for a septic wound and which he has not bothered to sterilise. There is no point in giving the instruments a brief brush under tap water: they should be stood in some kind of sterilising fluid. Tablets are easily available now that the majority of human babies are fed on the bottle, and cleaning the relevant apparatus requires nothing more than a few tablets or a bottle of cleansing solution. At the very least, instruments should be stood for a few seconds in boiling water and the hands washed in antiseptic soap.

If a wound requires stitching it should be done as soon as possible after the accident, but it must be remembered that stitching a deep wound may prevent dirt from getting out. When stitching is undertaken the lowest part of a wound should always be left open as a drain.

The most troublesome wounds are those which may best be described as punctures. They are almost always deep and there is only a very small surface area. The aperture must on no account be allowed to close and the inside of the wound must be syringed out frequently.

Wounds must heal from the inside towards the outside; if the outside heals first the wound is certain to become septic. For this reason alone, it is a mistake to apply any form of healing substance during the initial stages.

Books written between the wars tell hunt staff to look out for hysteria but modern research shows that it is not a disease in itself and that the kennelman should look for the real reasons. The symptoms seem to run through a whole pack merely from suggestion. C. B. Shepherd recorded the following:

> I have seen the pack assembled in the paddock, joyously awaiting their morning exercise, when one suddenly started to run round and round in large circles, snapping in the air and running into anything that came in his way. The others looked on evidently utterly shocked, and, by the time we had caught and removed the hysterical one, two more had followed his example . . . It is a most distressing complaint, and a hound that is badly affected may damage himself seriously in rushing about wildly and dashing his head against obstructions.

Hysteria has been attributed to many causes, from fleas to wireless waves, but one thing which has been noticed is that attacks diminish in intensity and frequency when foods abundant in vitamin A are supplied. Perhaps hysteria-type ailments are due to stomach disorders? A lack of vitamin A is definitely a serious deficiency as it is important for growth, eye development, bone, skin and the mucous membranes.

Poison problems

It should not be necessary to point out that all obvious poisons around the kennel premises must be kept under lock and key but there are many less obvious sources which may prove fatal. A hound is more likely to pick up some of the non-caustic poisons during the course of a hunting day and it would not be silly to suggest that a member of the hunt staff should carry with him at all times a small piece of washing soda in case of accidents.

Some of the most common forms of non-caustic poisons are strychnine put out for moles, agricultural chemicals, dressed seed and antifreeze. It might be argued that no dog in its right senses would willingly lap up the latter but it is not generally known that antifreeze is in fact very sweet tasting and, judging by the entries in many veterinary day-books, is a regular source of poisoning.

Caustic poisoning is a different proposition and a hound suffering from the effects of this type of discomfort should not be given washing soda in order to induce vomiting because the passage of the poison back through the trachea and soft palate will re-aggravate the situation. Instead, the poison should be diluted whilst in the stomach by giving milk in the case of an acidic poison or, for those of an alkaline nature, a solution of vinegar or lemon juice.

In all cases, the idea is to prevent absorption into the bloodstream and is only an intermediate measure before seeking professional help.

Likely caustic poisons are kerosene, battery acid, barbiturates and acetic acids. If the poison has not been taken internally, and is only on the skin or feet for instance, there is no need to panic but, nevertheless, a careful eye should be kept on the hound in case it begins to lick off the poison before there is any chance of washing it off.

Apart from poisoning, cuts are the most likely form of emergency to occur on the hunting day and they should be dealt with by placing a high-pressure bandage over the actual bleeding point before taking the hound for stitching at the surgery.

Obviously there should be a medicine box situated in the kennels and one in the hound van. There is no reason why the contents should not be suitable for both humans and hounds but, heartless though it might sound, the beagles should take precedence! A typical box will contain an antiseptic solution and cream such as

Savlon, which has a great advantage over many other antiseptics: it has long been accepted by grooms in racing and foxhunting establishments that, after a hard day, horses should be washed over with Savlon to sterilise any unnoticed small cuts and wounds without drying out the surrounding skin. The same has been found with dogs and with hounds in particular.

Bandages, pads of melolin (non-adhesive gauze) and waterproof sticking plaster should be kept and periodically checked, together with worming tablets, flea powder or spray such as Nuvan Top and, of course, a strong disinfectant.

Kennel life in the winter

As the hunting season approaches we have seen that hound exercise is increased and is of a more serious nature. During the autumn and winter it will be almost impossible for the pack which hunts two or more days a week to be able to give hounds any more than a daily run in the grass yards and it is doubtful whether they need more than this once they have had some serious hunting.

Maintenance of the buildings continues despite fewer hours of daylight in which to do it: wear and tear on the kennels have no respect of seasons. Hounds chew and bite their benches and projections in the kennels; timber rots; wire rusts. All these have to be replaced immediately — there is no way that one can wait until the main spring offensive.

Cutting up the meat and skinning and boning the casualties is likely to take up even more time as farmers begin to lose more livestock with the winter months. It also entails more time spent in riding around collecting from the farms.

On the hunting morning itself the feeding of the hounds which are not being hunted is usually carried out before vanning the rest. Food also has to be prepared for the rest of the pack on their return from hunting as obviously they cannot do their best on full stomachs.

Huntsmen vary enormously in their methods of feeding a pack after its return from hunting. A certain number will not feed until they have been back for an hour or more; others feed as soon as they get in. The latter would appear to be the most reasonable method and hounds should then be looked over for cuts and wounds before allowing them into the lodges to dry off.

Because straw provides a home for parasites, many huntsmen prefer to leave their hounds on bare benches without bedding. Indeed some hounds will express their dislike of straw by scratching it out on to the floor, but after a hard day's hunting they should be given the chance to roll in straw and dry themselves off. If straw is not liked in the benches, perhaps an old shed or spare lodge could be kept filled with clean, dry straw during the winter months and the hounds turned in there for a time to dry off. Another alternative to straw, if it can be acquired, is wood shavings or even shredded newspaper, both of which have excellent absorbent qualities and are not as attractive to fleas and lice.

At the beginning of the day, time will have to be allocated for deciding which hounds are to be taken and, unless it is a particularly small pack where all but the sick and dying are included, the drawing of hounds is often a time-consuming affair. There may be a reason why a young beagle should not be taken to a particular meet or there may be doubts about a certain hound's attitude towards sheep. Where bitches and dogs are kept separately, it will be necessary to draw equal proportions of the sexes. Most masters agree on the necessity for a mixed pack as this seems more reliable and encourages better drive. A bitch-only pack tends to be a little 'flighty'. When there is lameness in the kennels, possibly due to hunting over frosty ground, hounds suffering thus obviously have to be left at home.

Hygiene may be more difficult in winter, especially a hard one when water pipes, taps and drains freeze up and even the drinking troughs need constant de-frosting, and fresh water has to be carried by the bucketful.

So, even from the brief résumé of kennel life in winter, it can be seen that a certain ex-master of a university pack had his tongue in his cheek when I asked him what preparations his hunt staff carried out on the morning of the hunting day and he replied, 'I think my staff are usually out of bed by 11 if it is a 12 o'clock meet!'

Life in the kennels, summer or winter, is a labour of love and a matter for job satisfaction rather than for any financial remuneration and there is no doubt that there is satisfaction in seeing puppies which have been bred at the kennels, go out to walk, return and be useful members of the pack, both on and off the hunting field.

7

BREEDING, PUPPY WALKING
AND ENTRY

Even if it were possible to procure the best bitch in the country and
take it to the best stallion hound in the world, there is no guarantee
that any of the resultant litter would be any better than the majority
of hounds to be found in any beagle kennel situated around the
British Isles.

Selecting the right hound

Usually the kennel huntsman or the huntsman himself is responsible for the breeding policy; most masters realise that these people
know more about the pack than anyone else and, while there are no
hard and fast rules as to the make and shape of a beagle, there are
certain requirements that are more or less generally accepted as
being desirable. The points of a hound have already been discussed
in the chapter 'A Hound to Hunt the Hare' but individual tastes will
vary and some people, no matter whether the country dictates a
need for small hounds or large, will disregard any common-sense
formulas in favour of personal preference.

With the financial situation today, it is no longer possible for
those responsible to adopt the attitude of Lord Henry Bentinck
who, when asked the secret of his success with regard to foxhound
breeding, replied, 'I breed a great many; I put down a great many'.
Beagle kennels can only afford to breed a certain amount of litters
each year and each mating should be carried out with a view to the
future.

There are no definite rules and I have two books on the subject of hound breeding open in front of me. Both are written by 'experts', well qualified to put pen to paper, and yet they differ in their opinions. One tells the reader that he should:

> ... be careful to select as parents, both dog and bitch with a line of ancestry as nearly as possible of the height at which you are aiming ... it is unwise to breed from hounds lacking in symmetry and beauty, however well they perform ... Of the two, I consider the dog of far the greater importance ...

Whilst the second states that:

> Many breeders are prone to select their bitches rather at random, though they pay ever so much attention to the stallion hound to which they put them. This must be a mistake, as the bitch probably plays at least as big a part in the make-up of the progeny as does the dog.

Dog or bitch, which is the most important? From the above, people's opinions obviously differ but it should be remembered that the ideal is to acquire a level pack which hunts together.

It is necessary to have some knowledge of the rules of heredity and breeding. The hound list should be closely studied; in a long-established pack there will probably be the old and well-proven kennel lines and these are a good foundation on which to build all future hopes. It is not unusual to find the whole of an old-established kennel going back to one or two bitches, but those who are building up a pack should try to collect several female lines and keep them going for as long as possible, for the more there are, and the more different ways back there are to them, the closer it is possible to breed to the home kennel.

There is often some confusion as to the differences between in-breeding, line breeding and outcrossing.

Outcrossing is probably the most common method of breeding amongst beaglers and when a bitch which most conforms to the hunt's ideal comes in season she is usually taken to another hunt kennel which is known to have a good stallion hound on the premises for mating. If it is intended to use the same dog hound on more than one bitch during the same breeding season, then it is possible that the masters of the hunt to which the dog belongs will suggest that he goes to the bitches' kennels for a month or two.

It would be an unwise person who uses a dog hound unseen and purely from recommendation. Acquiring and studying the hound's pedigree is not enough and it is necessary to ensure that the animal is a good worker and free from fault. If possible, a visit to the kennels prior to the intended 'marriage' should be arranged and some of his offspring examined to see whether he breeds true to type. Of course difficulties arise when the dog is kennelled at the other of the country and, because of the time and expense involved, notes may have to be taken and the bitch ferried to the dog hound 'on spec'. During the course of the inevitable telephone calls to arrange the visit, some of the hound's points are bound to be discussed and if it is found that his own kennel uses him on their own bitches then it can be assumed that he is at least a good worker.

Irrespective of whether outcrossing, line breeding or inbreeding is being followed, it has become evident from the experiences of hound breeders that neither a bitch nor a dog hound should be bred from until they have finished at least two hunting seasons. No matter how well they have performed during their first season, there is always the chance that a fault or vice not yet noticed will become apparent in its second season as the hound's confidence grows. If the problem was then inherited and these hounds were subsequently bred from, then, as the generations continue, the problem will become greatly magnified.

Because of the regular input of fresh blood, outcrossing tends to increase the animals' stamina but reduces the purity of the blood and therefore its homogeneity, certain dominant characeristics of which are often desired. However if, for instance, the huntsman wishes to improve the nose and hunting ability of the whole of his pack, there is no point in using his own dog hound purely and simply because he is the same colour as the intended brood bitch: he must send the bitch to a kennel with a reputation for showing good sport on bad scenting country. The resultant offspring should have renewed vigour and freshness, as well as retaining the characteristics of the home strain.

Line breeding involves the mating between related hounds in an attempt to increase or concentrate the homogeneous qualities of a few individuals. Unless carefully controlled it is not long before line breeding becomes inbreeding, a most undesirable practice which brings to the surface bad characteristics more than it does good ones and also tends to lower stamina, resistance to disease, and decreases size and bone structure. The closer inbreeding is practised, the more likely it is that these failures will develop and the hunting ability will suffer as a result.

When carrying out line breeding, it is even more important than usual to study the hunt's stud books as, next to the selection of the actual sires and dams, choosing those hounds with the right sort of ancestry is vital if the venture is to be successful. If those ancestors are known to be without fault or vice and are capable of reproducing certain characteristics both mental and physical which, when mated to another hound, are then passed on and if the next generation also breeds true to type, then the breeder can mate the bitches in his kennels today which bear the names of those hounds of the past in their pedigrees with sires which also have them. In order to avoid inbreeding, however, those names should not appear nearer than four generations back. So, basically, the foundation sires and bitches should be the same throughout the whole pack and breeding should be carried out from those hounds with more or less the same ancestors.

The importance of possessing a thorough knowledge of all the forebears cannot be overestimated: if a certain characteristic is recessive for a number of years, it might be supposed that the breeder no longer needs to worry about its recurrence in the present generation of offspring, but if both dog and bitch possess genes which carry the same recessive characteristic and are then mated together there is a good likelihood that, although it has remained dormant for several years, the fault will reappear in a future generation.

It is no easy matter to breed good hounds; there is no short cut to success and there are bound to be a good many disappointments. However, over the years it will be possible to forecast a pattern which will strengthen the stock, eliminate weaknesses, determine size and colour and ensure 'huntability'.

Birth and after-care

As far as the actual care of a bitch in whelp is concerned, there is no real need to go into any great depth. Any book on the general welfare of dogs will advise the reader and, after all, the way in which a puppy is formed and born differs not in the slightest no matter whether the parents be chihuahua, wolfhound or beagle.

After the puppies are born, however, their treatment in the hunt kennels is likely to differ from that of puppies in the hands of an in-

A beagle bitch with day-old pups

dividual breeder who rears one litter every so often.

It is advisable to inject a brood bitch before she is mated so that she can pass on to her puppies immunity which will then last until about twelve weeks, when they can be given individual injections. It is doubtful whether the advice given in pencil at the end of a book in my possession, written in 1915, will suffice. As an aid to preventing distemper in a brood bitch or her litter, the unknown scribe recommends that one should 'leave a bowl of greasy, soapy dish-water by the dog's side. This has never failed to prevent'!

As an aside to this comment, it has long been thought that disinfectants used around the lodge in which the bitch is due to whelp should not contain carbolic or similar ingredients which irritate the mucous membranes. Although it may seem improbable, modern veterinary research shows that it is just possible that the use of carbolics may lead to whelps being 'slipped'.

Warmth is important to the bitch and her quarters should be insulated and draught free. An infra-red lamp strung up over the whelping box is a good idea when a litter is due in the early part of the year — a practice which most hunts try to achieve, for puppies born in February, March, April and May will have the benefits of the summer months. Sun is essential for thriving litters and when they are six months old in October they will be able to withstand the winter without undue hardship and be ready to enter at the start of the following season when they are around eighteen months old.

Straw (provided that it is clean) also helps in creating warmth, but, perhaps more importantly, because of its springiness it will help to prevent the bitch from squashing her puppies. Equally effective is the use of a low-sided, roomy box which has a guard rail fitted inside 2 inches up from the bottom and out from the side.

The nursing bitch needs to be fed lavishly and well, with the diet including some form of mineral supplement. Without such a safeguard, the bitch's supply of calcium may become so depleted as to cause fits, ending in coma and death.

One should take extreme care with the use of vitamins, however, and their over-use can cause as many, if not more, problems as their lack of use. Vitamins D and E, for instance, should never need to be added to a dog's diet. In the case of vitamin D, dogs generally make their own and to feed a supplement could well cause problems with fertility. Vitamin E is important to the brood bitch, being responsible for muscular development and to aid fertility, but a balanced diet should be free of any deficits.

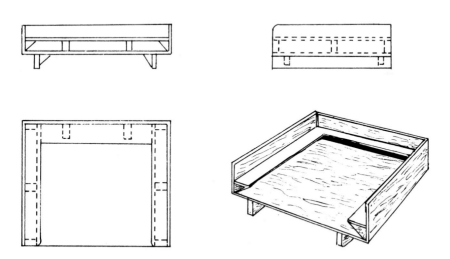

Front elevation, side elevation, plan and overall view of a whelping box, suitable not only for the beagle pack but also for the family dog. Especially important is the provision of a guard rail in order to prevent the brood bitch lying on any of her newly-born puppies; perhaps plenty of straw would serve the same purpose?

There is some doubt amongst dog breeders in general as to how many pups the bitch should be allowed to keep. Nowhere is the size of a litter more important than in the hound kennels. With several litters in the lodges at one time, supplementary feeding of those pups which cannot avail themselves of the bitch's milk (either due to failure of the bitch to produce enough milk or to the number of pups in a litter) will be impossible. The litter should therefore be confined to not more than five or six and the numbers reduced at about three days old. At this stage the only way on which to base a choice of which to keep and which to discard is on the basis of sex, colour and size. It needs a confident person to carry out such an operation; one of the destroyed pups might have turned out to be the pack leader but, in an effort to benefit the rest, individuals may have to be sacrificed. Very occasionally it may be possible to pass on puppies from one bitch to another with only three or four puppies of the same age.

Although some hunts feel that several hundred pounds spent at the vet's surgery is a waste of money, the majority of masters, and huntsmen, feel that all the puppies should be inoculated without fail at twelve weeks and then given annual booster shots.

Worming should be carried out between the sixth and eighth weeks and as each puppy is dosed it should be put in a separate place. With a number of animals, it is surprisingly easy to forget which have been treated and which have not.

Those young hounds which have been bred by a recognised hunt are eligible to be entered in the stud book compiled annually by the Association of Masters of Harriers and Beagles provided that they are the progeny of stud-book hounds on both sides or the progeny of a stud-book hound and an appendix hound. The procedure is described in rule two of the association's *Rules for Stud Books:*

> Young hounds should be registered in the stud book by the master or the official representative of the hunt which bred them, irrespective of whether they have been sold or given away; and such entries must reach the honorary secretary by the date specified with such fee as shall have been determined pursuant to rule seven. Hounds which have not been registered as young hounds may be registered in subsequent years, the annual closing date for such entries being March the first, and the fee payable for a late entry shall be at the same rate as, but in addition to, the fee payable for an entry of young hounds.

Rule five states that:

The name of a registered hound which has been transferred to another hunt must always be preceded by the name of the hunt which registered it.

Puppy walkers

As soon as the necessary courses of injections and medical require-ments have been carried out at the kennels, most hunts like to send the year's puppies out to walk and there can be no doubt that hounds which have had the benefit of an alternative education to that which is offered at the kennels do much better when the time comes to enter them to the hunting pack.

There can sometimes be a problem in finding suitable candidates who are prepared to take puppies from the kennels and look after them from the age of twelve weeks until the following spring. The problem varies from area to area.

In some there is no shortage of good walks, places where the pups can run about all day long in complete safety and where they will be well cared for. Although beagle puppies have been walked in the most unlikely places — a London flat and exercise in Hyde Park for instance — obviously if hounds can be placed with local farmers and landowners, so much the better. They should also, however, ideally be situated in the hunt's own country and any subscriber to a particular hunt who happens to live in the country of a 'rival' pack and who wishes to walk a puppy or two should make sure that the masters have first obtained the consent of the master of that country if ill feeling is to be avoided.

For those people considering walking puppies for the first time, perhaps the reasons why hounds are sent out to walk at all should be outlined. Basically, the puppy will see more of life and thus be more confident. To achieve this in the kennels a huntsman or kennelman would need to spend most of his time with an indi-vidual hound and this is obviously an impossible task when there are another thirty or forty hounds needing his urgent attention. The puppy walker on the other hand, with only one or two puppies to consider, can spend much of his time during the early months of a puppy's life making the dog confident and generally obedient.

It should be remembered that, although the aim of any kind of training is to control the bodily actions, this can only be effected through the medium of the dog's mind. It is, therefore, the mind and not the body of the dog with which the puppy walker should be primarily concerned.

Each hound has a particular character and disposition and in a litter it will be noticed at a very early age that one dog is shy, one docile, one wilful, one highly strung and another responsive. Each must be treated with these characteristics in mind if, at the end of the day, the puppy walker is going to return a mature, well-mannered beagle to the kennel.

Puppy psychology

During the early stages, the brood bitch will be the centre of interest to pups which have yet to be weaned. After weaning, the feed dish will take the place of the dam and at this stage the hound will be delivered to the walker who will, purely through feeding and supplying individual attention, become the new and permanent centre of interest to the puppy.

As adolescence develops, hound pups will, quite naturally, find that the scents of the countryside and in particular that of game in one form or another will create a further centre of interest and to an extent this should be encouraged. But only to an extent and here it might be appropriate to include the well-worn saw, 'How long is a piece of string?'

The whole purpose of breeding the hound in the first place is in the fond hope that it will prove a useful hunter. But to a hound which runs riot on a rabbit on its first day out with the pack, how can you explain why such action was encouraged whilst out at walk? This natural development has therefore to be carefully controlled and the walker has to try and retain the position of chief centre of interest in the hound's mind whilst these hunting instincts are being developed without in any way retarding them. This is a prime example of the benefits of outside training against puppy walking in the kennels. Also, in the pack the members of the group are centres of interest to each other and will be less inclined later to acquiesce to the wishes of the huntsman, their behaviour being entirely different to that which is evident when dealing with only one.

There are many matters for which a knowledge of canine psychology will prove useful to the puppy walker and although he is not expected to provide a hound which is completely under his control, he should make the puppy come when it is called, be steady with all forms of livestock and be used to a collar.

A timid puppy may be reluctant to come when called but the person with dog sense will not chase the puppy about in an effort to catch him and either frighten him further or turn the whole thing into a game, but instead will run away from the dog, calling him up as he does so. The beagle, afraid of being left behind and curious to see what is happening, will then run after the walker, who can stoop down in order to make his bulk less frightening and make a big fuss of the puppy.

It is clearly useless to attempt to impart obedience to a puppy which does not answer to his name and from the very earliest days it should always be spoken to by the name given to it in the kennels. There is very little point in the puppy walker calling his charge by a pet name when the huntsman will expect it to answer to another on its return to the pack.

In the early stages edible rewards are useful in getting a hound puppy used to and interested in the walker, especially if its capacity for giving attention is impaired by an initial fear of its new 'foster' walker, However, as soon as giving a reward has had the desired effect, the practice should be stopped and fondling, combined with a few words of praise, should be sufficient to keep the beagle happy and responsive.

Whether punishment should be given is a moot point. Subscribers to a certain school of thought feel that any form of chastisement, other than that given whilst in a pack environment, will only serve to break the spirit of the hound.

Fifty years ago, the masters of packs of hounds (foxhounds in particular) were probably landowners and could almost insist that their tenants, farm workers and estate staff take on hounds for puppy walking. At that time these masters expected that the puppies would be given a completely free rein and would be allowed to chase anything or dig up the whole of the puppy walker's garden without any form of correction. Unstinted freedom at walk was felt to be as necessary for the puppy's moral education as it was for its physical welfare. The very act of ruining the garden was supposed to form part of its education and from this it would learn that a pile of barbed wire left in the corner of the farmyard would cut it, that a child's tennis ball chewed and digested would give it stomach ache, and that the gardener's bonfire, complete with yesterday's hot ashes, would not really form a comfortable place in which to rest. In theory these ideas seem very sound but one should also bear in mind that this was the era in the gundog world when dog breakers, as opposed to dog trainers, abounded and that their idea of canine physchology was to beat a recalcitrant dog until it either submitted or became so cowed that it had to be destroyed. Evidence of this school of thought is to be found in the old shooting story which originated at the turn of the century when the host of a shooting day turned to his head keeper and told him, 'After you have beaten the spaniels, we will make a start'.

Any dog, no matter what the breed, deserves better treatment than this and thankfully today's masters are prepared to do more than merely travel round potential puppy walkers advising them when to expect delivery; instead they realise the importance of a thorough grounding in dog management and, along with diet sheets, collars and other necessary paraphernalia, will advise on the form of correction during the training stage.

A bold puppy, which constantly irritates by doing wrong and which has had sufficient experience to know that it is in fact doing wrong, can often be successfully punished with a shaking and telling off. Sometimes the tone of voice alone is enough to convey to an intelligent hound that the misdemeanour has displeased his new owner but normally the puppy should be held by the slack skin under the throat or at the side of the neck and it should then be possible, with a dog of beagle size, to lift all four of its feet off the ground and give it a severe shaking whilst at the same time glaring into its eyes. The psychology behind this act is that the trainer or walker is reasserting his authority as leader of the pack. Watch two dogs fighting: nine times out of ten the dominant animal will attack that loose skin around the neck.

Whilst on the subject of punishment, one important point which must be mentioned is that, whatever form of correction has been decided upon, it should be given immediately the offence is committed and at the place where it was committed. A hound should never be punished when it comes up to the puppy walker and never, under any circumstances, after a period of time has elapsed.

The continual nagging of a hound will often only succeed in producing a beagle which has a total disregard of requests, commands or orders. If it is accompanied by punishment, of whatever kind, the animal will often become so accustomed to being judged in this

162

manner that it will no longer have any fear of the admonishment. Instead, a command should be given and instant obedience expected.

The puppy walker's responsibilities

The puppy walker should consider his own position before making any approaches to the kennels regarding taking puppies out to walk and he should consider carefully his own personality. Just because he has an obsessive interest in hound work, he will not necessarily make a good 'foster parent'. His topographical position is also important and, although we have already seen that it is possible to walk a beagle puppy in the centre of London and that it is no longer considered essential for hounds to have free range over a vast acreage of garden or estate, care must be taken in order to avoid walks where there is an ever-present risk, either from roads or from any other sources. A farming location might at first seem to be an ideal environment and from the point of view of accustoming hounds to the countryside and livestock, so it is, but when one examines the situation further other unforeseen problems begin to arise.

Farmers, being farmers, are likely to allow their puppies the freedom to which they would have been used fifty years ago and, other than shutting them in an empty loosebox for the night, will not be too concerned about their whereabouts for the rest of the day. In hot weather, however, dogs of any breed will seek the shade and on a farm this is likely to be in outbuildings or underneath machinery. Hot weather generally signifies the start of the farmer's busy seasons, that is silage, haymaking and harvest, when everyone is naturally in a rush to get the jobs done before the weather breaks. The backing into a shady shed or the hitching up of hitherto stationary machinery and then driving off could result in an injured or dead hound. Beagle pups must therefore be taken into account and locked up out of harm's way during the busy times.

If the hunt subscriber still wishes to take on puppies after considering all the potential pitfalls, he should give some thought to kennelling arrangements. This will depend to some extent on whether he is taking on a single hound or a couple.

Two puppies undoubtedly amuse each other and, as they are pack animals which are eventually going to be kennelled as part of a pack, taking on two beagles where circumstances permit is definitely preferable to one. On the de-merit side, however, it should be remembered that two dogs are more likely to go out looking for trouble and will require extra vigilance on the part of the puppy walker, especially in sheep country. Worrying usually starts out as a game between two or more young dogs; at first they want the sheep to play their game and as it runs away they give it one or two playful nips. Before long they are at its throat and the walker has to explain to an irate sheep farmer how the situation arose; the hunt acquires a bad reputation and, perhaps worst of all, a potentially brilliant hunting hound has to be destroyed.

To return to the kennelling arrangements: it may be decided to keep the beagles indoors but with this decision comes the possibility that the hounds will be allowed to become nothing more than lap-dogs. In any case it should still be made possible for the puppies to be kennelled for some part of the day, as although the whole purpose of putting hounds out to walk is to 'humanise' them, unless a responsible member of the household is around to keep the puppies under close scrutiny they will be better off in a good kennel.

Contrary to what the masters who insisted on giving a hound absolute freedom believed, any dog is happier with a stable home of

Originally used as gundog kennels and now obviously in a state of disrepair, this adapted pig-box could, with half a day's work, be made habitable for one or two beagle puppies out on a walk *(Regina Arnold)*

its own and, reinforcing an important point, will not have the opportunity to go off on its own hunting or foraging.

The sleeping accommodation need not be elaborate. An old packing case or barrel, with a board inside to form a flat floor and a piece of sacking hanging over the entrance to keep out draughts, will be sufficient. Ideally the edifice should be surrounded by a large area which is in turn fenced with chainlink or similar suitable material. The fencing need not be as high as that required for a grass run designed for adult beagles.

Farmers and establishments which cater for horses may have a loosebox or similar building to put at the disposal of the beagle pups and all that may then be necessary is for a sleeping bench to be included. Puppy benches should be almost at floor level and constructed so that it is possible to raise them as the puppies get older. The sudden jarring impact of jumping down from a height is liable to cause the front legs to become distorted and it is thought by many that benches which are too high are the cause of hounds being out at the elbows.

Knowing the propensity of puppies to chewing, I recommend that the side boards of a bench should be covered with tin or zinc sheeting; indeed, any projecting battening or surfaces are best covered in this way if one wishes to prevent unnecessary damage.

As to the size of the kennel, if a good-sized exercise run is available, suitable dimensions for a single hound would be around 4 feet square, the height at the front being the same. For a couple of hounds a kennel 6 feet by 4 feet with a frontage height of around 5 feet will be sufficient.

The feeding of the puppies will be the same as that for any other breed of dog. Because a dog is a carnivore and a scavenger, meat (and sometimes very smelly meat) would be its main diet in the wild. When wild animals have made a kill they usually eat the paunch of their victim first; the partially digested vegetable matter in the stomach provides vitamins and trace elements which would otherwise be absent from an all-meat diet. This must be remembered when planning the puppies' diet. Having had the bacterial contents of raw meat explained to me in great detail, I hesitate to suggest that meat being prepared for puppies should be fed raw but many successful dog breeders state that there is no need to cook it or even cut it up. If, as I feel, cooking is preferred, the cooking should not be prolonged. The liquid in which the meat is cooked should also be fed to the puppy as it contains the minerals (but not the bacteria) in the food. The meat should not be minced or ground and left open to the elements for any period of time because this destroys the vitamin content.

The idea that a puppy should not have fat is a mistaken one: fat is quite beneficial, provided that it is given in reasonable proportion. Offal and fish are very good but should not be given more than once a week. Canned food is convenient but has the disadvantage of being expensive; if the puppy walker decides to use tinned meat he must ensure that it is recommended by the manufacturers as being suitable for young puppies.

The rest of the diet can be made up of scraps and dog biscuits. Biscuit meal served soggy is bad for the puppies' teeth if given without any variation. Whatever the feed, the hunt kennels are often able to supply a puppy walker who lives close by with meat, porridge or biscuit, essentials which will cut down considerably on the personal costs involved.

Beagles on a coupling: an excellent arrangement for acclimatising a young hound to his elders and betters, or when walking a couple of puppies together

Cod-liver oil is beneficial to the growing puppies as is the inclusion of yeast tablets, which provide the B complex of vitamins.

The amount of food needed by each dog will vary but a rough guide is to give as much as the hound will eat in ten minutes or, alternatively, 2/3 of an ounce of food per pound of the dog's body-weight.

At the age of nine weeks, beagle pups should be receiving four meals a day, broken down into cereal and milk-based foods, with a main meal of meal and biscuits. By the age of four months, the feeds should have been reduced to three meals a day, a routine which is continued until around eight months, after which two meals a day should be sufficient to ensure the puppies' well-being.

At any age, a big bone which will not splinter helps to improve the development of the teeth and will also help to keep the puppy amused.

When a couple of puppies are being walked together, the kennels may send a leather coupling with them and if the puppy walker can get his hounds used to it the next stage of their education when they return to the pack will be made that much easier.

Entering the young hounds

As the young beagles return from walk, they are usually kennelled separately from the main pack and gradually introduced to the entered hounds during hound exercise. There will, however, be a short time before exercise begins in earnest and, until then, the young entry should be walked out separately from the pack. Whenever possible this exercise should be undertaken by the person who will eventually hunt them. It is more likely that any exercise during the first month or two will only consist of that obtained by being let loose into the grass runs but, even so, the huntsman must not lose any opportunity to take a pocketful of biscuit and spend a few minutes each day with the young hounds, calling them up to him by name and making a fuss of them. At this stage he should not worry too much if they jump up at him as the whole point of these precious few minutes is to allow the hounds plenty of opportunity to transfer their affections from the puppy walker to the huntsman. Under no circumstances should he lose his temper with the puppies, for if he does he will probably destroy any confidence that has been built in the hounds' minds. In fact it is probably better for the huntsman not to go near the puppies at all when he has had a disagreement with his wife or a difference of opinion with someone around the kennels and there is the chance that his bad mood might be aggravated by the overplayful activities of a young entry. In such a mood one is liable to do something which the puppy does not understand.

At all times the huntsman should not forget the ultimate objective: that of getting a fully competent hound into the hunting field. Although it might require some sweet talking on the part of the master if he is called upon to explain to a puppy walker why his hound has been drafted (always drafted, never destroyed!), a careful eye should be kept on all the young hounds and any which have got this far but which will obviously not benefit the hunt any further should be removed. But be careful: it does not do to discard an apparently unpromising puppy too early, for often the slow starters end up as the best mature workers. A sensitive hound has brains and eventually finishes up a brilliant worker. A stolid puppy, on the other hand, whilst easier to train and far less worry to begin with, often (but not always) ends up as a mediocre worker or one which will riot at the slightest provocation. The difficult, sensitive puppy which has learnt a lesson will not forget it easily and is more likely to excel in the field than its stolid brother.

A good and experienced puppy walker will already have assessed the character of each hound in his care and will be able to pass on his observations to the kennels, thus saving them much time when it comes to working out the mentality of an individual beagle and the time required in preparing it for the serious duties of hunting.

As with most aspects of beagling, how the puppies are introduced to the rest of the pack differs slightly from hunt to hunt but a practice which seems to be widespread is that of coupling an unentered hound with one which is in its fifth season and which can teach the puppy to obey the commands of the huntsman. Alternative methods are to couple two puppies together or on two couplings fixed to a single hound.

The time taken to accustom these hounds to exercising with the established members of the pack will depend on each puppy and they should always be assessed on an individual basis. It may take two weeks or two months for a particular pup to realise that it is now part of a pack but there is no great rush: do not worry if hounds are still 'puppyish'. Once they are settled, however, they should be allowed out singly and watched carefully to see that they do not develop any undesirable habits.

When the unentered hounds are used to the pack, the final part of their education will come from the hunting day. The usual plan of entering pups is by means of early morning hunts, thus taking full advantage of the fact that the ground will still be damp with dew and therefore more likely to hold a scent. Also, the hares perhaps will be a little less on their toes after a successful night of feeding than they might otherwise be.

Early hunting lessons

Early morning bye-days are sometimes used as a means of getting hounds fit rather than to enter puppies but there is no real reason why the two objectives should not be combined. After all, they can only learn their trade by instinct and example, neither of which is possible if they are left behind in kennels.

Where September bye-days are fixed, as the beagling equivalent of cub-hunting, every effort should be made to meet on ground which is known to carry a good stock of hares and if possible the young hounds should be allowed to get away on a well-grown leveret rather than an old experienced hare, the catching of which will seem an impossible task to puppies still unsure of themselves. The whole point of the game is to encourage the young entry and when they go back to the kennels they should feel that the scent of the hare is the basis of fun and excitement. They should not be kept out so long as to get tired and disillusioned. Indeed a disadvantage with an early morning meet is that if one hunts too long the sun gets higher, the ground drier and the hounds hotter. During August and September the country is almost certain to be very hot and scentless from about ten o'clock onwards, and hunting under such conditions can do nothing to improve either the physique or morale of the young entry.

A way to overcome this would be to take hounds out at the other end of the day but, no matter what the timing, there should not be too much publicity amongst subscribers as to where and when the meet is to be held, for this early hunting is purely for the sake of the hounds and the master's consideration for his subscribers comes nowhere at all. No money should be taken in the way of a 'cap', for then the huntsman would feel he was under some kind of obligation to show some sport in return for the money. Those who do attend should be those who can be relied upon to help when hounds are experiencing difficulty and no one who watches hounds carefully in their work can fail to notice just how much that work is affected by a series of disappointments. With a good scent the hounds will, of course, go fast and drive along well and people lucky enough to attend these early preliminaries to the season will find immense pleasure in seeing it done in good style.

A choice between morning and evening is an easy one and without a doubt the early morning meet is the most enjoyable; there is the thrill of being around whilst others are still in bed, observing wildlife which is not easily seen at any other time of the day and, perhaps best of all, the huge breakfast waiting to be consumed on your return, plus the knowledge that, although you have been out enjoying yourself for several hours, there is still a full day ahead.

A final point regarding the suitability of the meet when it is primarily planned for the entry of young hounds: from personal experience, I know that a hare does go to ground at times, usually towards the end of the hunt when she is hard pressed. Although it may seem supercilious to state that this is a fact known to few, and perhaps doubted by many who have not seen it, fact it is and it probably happens more often than is known. In the sixteenth century in particular, writers on hare hunting gave the animal credit for marvellous cunning, which undoubtedly she has, but perhaps it was her ability to go to ground without anyone's knowledge that helped to establish the belief in the hare's ability to disappear without trace and thus led her to be considered supernatural, capable of turning herself into another form. An area which is known to facilitate the hiding of a hare and which leaves very little scent is not conducive to satisfying the hunting instinct of a young beagle.

Before long, provided that the breeding, walking and entry have been correctly carried out, in the words of G. J. Whyte-Melville (in 'Drink, Puppy, Drink'):

> The pack is staunch and true, now they run from scent to view,
> And it's worth the risk of life and limb and neck, boys;
> To see them drive and stoop till they finish with 'Who Whoop'.
> Forty minutes on the grass without a check, boys.

8
BEAGLING IN THE EIGHTIES

The problems of beagling today

A chapter of this nature has probably never before been really necessary in a book dealing with any aspect of fieldsports but, with political parties hoping to catch votes by banning any form of 'hunting with dogs', all fieldsports bar fishing seem to be at risk. It is therefore in everyone's interest to show a humane and caring front.

The shooting man should ensure that his quarry is killed cleanly and that the inevitable wounded bird or animal is quickly found and cleanly dispatched. There are ways of killing a bird aesthetically without having to resort to first stunning it to death against a tree or fence or swinging it round by the head until, more by luck than good management, the neck breaks and the subject could be classed as clinically dead.

Hunting has a certain advantage: the quarry is either killed quickly and efficiently by a nip from a hound in the neck or back, which means an instant death, or gets well away from its pursuers, tired, but well able to recover and continue the normal course of day-to-day living.

At some time or another, even the beagler will be subjected to a tirade of abuse which, although it may stem from a person who is usually vitriolic and uninformed, must be treated with reason and not a stream of four-letter words.

I remember fifteen years ago being called a 'bloody sadist' and, apart from knowing the difference between 'sadist' and 'masochist', had no idea of why the word had been used. Under no circumstances did I consider myself to be a person who enjoyed the suffering of others. To me beagling was a way of being involved with animals which worked for a living and used their basic instincts rather than being merely pampered pets. Gundogs, sheepdogs or hounds of any nature were all the same to me.

Obviously all living creatures are frightened by pain but I venture to suggest that it is only *Homo sapiens* who possess the knowledge and imagination to anticipate death and the events leading up to it. An animal's fear of death only occurs when death is a second or two away and it then knows that its demise is imminent, purely and simply because it knows there is no way that it can get away from the situation.

To a lesser or greater degree, everybody hunts. As soon as a mouse is seen in the kitchen of an ordinary household, the first reaction is to get rid of it. There is no pleasure attached to the operation, which is looked upon as getting rid of a pest which, if left unattended, will chew through packets of food and probably increase its numbers.

To the uninformed, then, this behaviour is tolerated but for someone actually to enjoy killing for the sake of it seems to them to be totally unacceptable. If beaglers ventured into the field merely to see a hare caught and killed, then their morals and mentality must indeed be in question. Writing from experience, I have on at least a dozen occasions followed otterhounds, seen countryside quite different from that in which I work and have had the pleasure of viewing an otter at close quarters, a sight which would otherwise have been denied to me. Never once did the hounds kill but this did not make me any less eager to take up an opportunity of going out with hounds again. I made new friends, saw a red kite hunting in the Welsh mountains and once, during an obligatory stop at a village pub on the way home, was treated to the rehearsals of a prominent Welsh male voice choir!

It is said that the hunting instinct lies dormant in most of today's civilisations and an early dictionary definition of sport is: 'A pastime afforded by the endeavour to take or kill wild animals'. As civilisation grew and flourished, the city populations became too large for more than a small proportion, usually the rich and powerful, to indulge in hunting as a pastime rather than as a necessity. Hunters set out to test their skill against prey that were no longer essential to their well-being. The kill may still have been consumed (with the notable exception of Oscar Wilde's 'unspeakable in pursuit of the uneatable') but there were a good many easier ways of ensuring a good meal and the chase became exposed as an end in itself.

Often those who do not agree with hunting attack the somewhat archaic appearance of the hunt uniform, but it has, in the main, been evolved for purely untilitarian purposes — more so with foxhunters than beaglers, it must be admitted, but nevertheless most items of apparel remain practical. Even if they were not, the hunt uniform differs only slightly from that worn by show-jumping enthusiasts and who has ever levelled such an argument against them? And where is the practicality in wearing 'whites' to play cricket when, as everyone who has ever washed a pair of flannels knows, grass stains are almost impossible to remove?

A brief discourse such as the above does, I hope, help the reader to clarify his argument against those who question his sport. How best to deal with the presence of anti-fieldsport groups during the hunting day is left until the end of the chapter because certain packs are more troubled than others, and other more widespread problems deserve first mention.

It is interesting to note that sporting writers at the turn of the century viewed the advent of the motor vehicle as being a nail in the coffin of hunting. Some were cautious in extolling the virtues of arriving at the meet in cars and 'could not deny the comforts of the proceeding'. As Commander Forbes noted:

> There were few meets that could not be reached by the wonder-working vehicle in half an hour. Therefore there was no hurry about breakfast, toilet, correspondence, or the digestion of the morning papers, and I could see no objection to the arrangement. We met with no accident, ran over no pig nor dog, crawling child not any other creeping thing; we startled no animals badly and, I trust, scandalised none of His Majesty's lieges.

Yet, disliking change and modernisation, Forbes felt compelled to finish his paragraph with: 'But, when all is said and done, I prefer the hack'.

Undoubtedly the motor car has affected hunting but not necessarily in the way that the early twentieth-century foxhunters saw it. Their main concern was that it would 'frighten the horses' and it is easy to imagine the amazement of Commander Forbes who in 1908 '. . . saw at a meet . . . five motor cars grouped amongst the hounds and hunt servants, and some of the horses were actually touching the motors, all of which had full steam up. A photograph was taken of the scène . . . The group was arranged to show how horses can be got to accommodate themselves to these monsters which have now taken possession of our roads . . .'

All horses and no mention of hounds who, after all, provide the mainstay of sport, whether it be staghunting, foxhunting or beagling. Dogs of any nature can in fact be assumed to have become used to traffic through the generations until, for the most part, today they are endowed with a certain natural road sense.

No, the real problem with hunting today while related to the advent of the car concerns instead the availability of country over which to hunt. There is, I believe a rule (maybe unwritten) which suggests that a meet should not be held within 2 miles of a major road. If I am mistaken and have dreamt it, then perhaps there should be one! It is courting disaster to hunt near busy highways. It will not necessarily be the hare which takes hounds into the danger zone but, with deer numbers apparently on the increase in most areas, a roebuck causing beagles to riot could mean an unexpected excursion close to or even over the road. Traditional meets may have to be rearranged but such precautions are obviously preferable to several couple of dead hounds. When hounds are hunting they are, we hope, hunting as a pack and because they are close together casualties in the case of either a road or railway accident will be high.

I have, I know, been guilty of labouring the dangers of roads and railways throughout this book but I have a particular fear of both, having seen quantities of good hounds killed within seconds. When this happens the hunt suffers not only their immediate loss but also a more long-term effect with regard to their breeding policy. Accidents take years to get over and, although not connected with either road or rail, when the Aldershot Beagles lost several couple of hounds over a quarry face in 1976, it took a decade or more for the masters and huntsman to achieve the quality of pack which they had before the disaster.

Many hunts have amalgamated due to the loss of good hunting country through road and rail development. It is unlikely that any of today's packs will be as lucky with transport as they were in the days of the steam train. There is an eye-witness report of an incident in the history of the Clifton Foot Beagles in 1898:

The hare had run the line, and two or three couples of hounds got away after her, running merrily straight down between the metals to an approaching luggage train. The engine passed over them, and the whole train after it, but, strange to say, when it had passed, the hounds were unhurt, and still running in full cry.

General urban development poses natural problems as do any changes in local agricultural practices. Intensive cereal farming, which involves the removal of long-established grass leys and hedgerows in order to allow the new 'agribusiness' methods of 'get rich quick' operators, prove to have had an effect on the hare and obviously it is fruitless to hold a meet in a vicinity where no hares abound.

The hedges have, in many cases, been replaced with artificial fencing and, more importantly from the hunting point of view, sheep neeting. The repeated use of this commodity in some countries has led the various hunts to breed somewhat larger beagles in order to be able to get over the fences, but, conversely, smaller hounds can surely be expected to scramble through the links?

A greater use of artificial fertilisers, diesel-powered machinery, and increased acreages of plough (notably poor scenting ground)

Hounds in full cry will find some way to overcome an obstacle. Over the gate, through barbed wire or over the inner perimeter of sheep netting is all the same to a pack on a strong scent

together with wire, heavy traffic and crowds have put the modern hound at a disadvantage and to be successful it needs to have the capability of turning even more tightly on the line of the quarry.

A growing number of landlords are preventing access to the hunt and a hostile smallholder, if positioned in the middle of prime hunting country, can ruin an otherwise good meet by refusing to allow the hunt on to his ground. Company pension schemes, mindful of their members' likely views on hunting, may also refuse entry, as may the local county council. During the last decade council bans have undoubtedly affected the activities of both hunter and shooter alike. Some of these bans have in fact been brought about as a direct result of pressure from the League Against Cruel Sports who, as part of their policies, request bans on not only council ground but also on some National Trust and Crown property.

Politics and how they affect fieldsports are probably best left alone in a book of this nature but it might be appropriate to mention to all who hunt, shoot or fish that whenever a general or by-election arises, it might be a good idea to establish a candidate's views in this matter. Manifestos and any other literature should be avidly read and any relevant points noted in readiness for drafting a letter. Any influence which the general public may have will only become apparent to a particular party or individual MP if many people write in order to state their point of view. The odd letter will invariably be dismissed as being the work of a 'crank' and not even worthy of an acknowledgement.

When it first became obvious in the mid-seventies that fieldsports were under possible attack, the British Field Sports Society showed great foresight in inaugurating a 'fighting fund'. As yet, the money from this successful venture appears to have been untouched. Let us hope that, when the crucial time arises, it will be used successfully.

Beagling is at a disadvantage in that its followers do not have the excuse that they are exterminating 'vermin' but it is unlikely that it will be the first sport to be abolished as it probably has a greater following than coursing or staghunting. Coursing is likely to be the first to fall, then staghunting, followed by beagling.

During the period 1950–1, the then Labour government made the decision to create a committee composed of a naturalist, zoologist, veterinary surgeon, practising doctor and representative from one of the trade unions in order to investigate the 'practices or activities which may involve cruelty to British wild animals'.

Known as the Scott Henderson Committee, it concluded that hunting with hounds was certainly the most humane method. It appears then that as yet neither 'Left', 'right' nor 'down the middle' can be held responsible for any decisions made and the whole business of fieldsports is still a matter for individuals in all the main political parties.

Anti-hunting groups and a brief history

A brief outline of the origins of the various groups which decry 'bloodsports' may give a little background information into their activities and what they are hoping to achieve when they turn up at the meet. Remember, everyone has the right to express their opinions and it is only when a group of objectors break the law and put hounds, hunt supporters, road users and often themselves at risk that action needs to be taken.

Probably the first organised opposition to hunting came with the formation of the Humanitarian League in 1891. Although founded by two RSPCA members, Messrs Salt and Williams, it was not primarily concerned with anti-hunting matters. The main method of attack came by publicity hand-outs and one of their first leaflets led an attack on the Royal Buckhounds and outlined the alleged cruelty involved with hunting the carted deer. (This was a very artificial operation, not much better than draghunting: often the deer was more of a pet kept in kennels and would run from its box at the meet, do the circuit and then return to the box of its own free will.) During the campaign it was pointed out that £6,000 was taken annually from the Civil List for the upkeep of the pack.

Flushed with success, in 1902 the league turned its attentions to the Eton College Beagles, at the time the only pack of beagles to be owned by a school or college. As the Eton College are still with us, it can only be assumed that this particular publicity campaign was unsuccessful.

In 1924 two former members of the Humanitarian League, Amos and Bell, felt that neither the league nor the RSPCA were doing enough to turn the public against hunting in general and they therefore formed the League for Prohibition of Cruel Sports, which is now known as the LACS (League Against Cruel Sports).

There are no accurate figures as to the membership of the league today but figures of 'around 12,000' were quoted at the start of this decade. It seems that legacies provide the league with more money than do subscriptions. During the same period, 62 per cent of the league's total income came from donations, whilst only 3 per cent was raised from members in the form of an annual fee. A further 8 to 10 per cent came from one-off donations, interest and the like.

By its own admission the League Against Cruel Sports uses a form of class antagonism if it can be turned to its advantage. According to interviews with three LACS members recorded in the early 1970s, when the society first began to pose a serious threat, although the popular image of a league supporter is of a long-haired, hippie-type leftie, converts were being recruited from 'urban middle-class people who know little about the details of hunting, but who abhor cruelty and violence and may, with luck, disapprove of privilege'.

Allied to its publicity, planned to show the 'privileged' classes at a disadvantage, the society deliberately in my opinion publicises incidents which put hunting in a bad light and have many times won psychological points in the press. For some reason most of these incidents seem, from the records available, to have occurred in the late sixties and early seventies.

The precedent set by the Humanitarian League in using passive means to generate publicity has, in the main, continued successfully to the present day but, at various points in the league's history, deviations have occurred. In 1958, for instance, false aniseed trails were first used in an effort to confuse hounds. A non-harmful deviation as it turns out, as is the modern practice of horn blowing. The same cannot be said of the appalling practice of spraying Anti-mate into the noses and eyes of hounds but all activities create publicity.

Sanctuaries were formed by the league (mainly in the West Country, where they usually affected staghunting) in order to deny access by 'undesirables'.

The year 1963 saw the foundation of the Hunt Saboteurs Association, a subsidiary of the league and founded by members who intended to disrupt hunting by less passive methods than placard carrying. Their publicity blurb stated that they wished to bring an end to hound sports by 'legal, non-violent, direct means and to bring to the attention of People and Parliament the barbaric cruelties involved in the hunting of animals until such time as these practices are banned by law'.

The methods involved were fourfold: firstly to keep the organisation informal, second to concentrate on disrupting hunts, thirdly to encourage other animal welfare organisations to press for a legislative change, and fourthly to remain just within the law. The first three aims are reasonable, the fourth perhaps a little doubtful, but nevertheless the number of 'hits' which a hunt may expect in a season will depend on the size and enthusiasm of its particular local group. Although mainly affecting foxhunting packs, such visits are not infrequently made to beagles. Some beaglers have the misfortune to be plagued every weekend for the whole of the hunting season; others only occasionally.

Just how often these visits occur depends on the hunt's proximity to built-up areas and the opinions of those who live there. That these opinions vary was a fact brought out in a survey carried out in the mid sixties by Christopher Fuller, who published his findings under the title *An Urban Survey of Views on Wildlife Conservation*. As a result of some very intensive research, the differences between Bristol (a large city) and Shrewsbury (a country town) became very obvious. In Bristol, 83 per cent thought hunting and shooting harmful, but only 55 per cent in Shrewsbury.

Avoiding trouble

One of the first requirements in avoiding the unwanted attentions of protesters, whether peaceful or otherwise, is to be careful when publicising any forthcoming meets or summer events. Meet cards should be sent only to paid-up members of the hunt and bona fide supporters. It is no longer possible to send off cards to the local press or to publicans in the vicinity, in case the information reaches the wrong hands. It just has to be accepted that fields may be down because of the inability to make public the intended meets. A quiet, uncomplicated hunting day is more important.

I think it was the Duke of Beaufort who first had the idea of advising hunt supporters by means of the telephone, an idea which seems to have caught on successfully with some beagle packs. Basically, hunt staff advise half a dozen or so committee members about Saturday's meet; the committee members in turn telephone another half a dozen followers and each of these then pick up the 'phone in order to tell another half dozen. These six telephone another six, and so on.

Police involvement

The hunt secretary must advise the police of the meet at least a week in advance so that, in areas where trouble is likely to occur, the station sergeant or whoever is in charge of planning the duty roster can allocate men to the area. It may seem an overdramatic move in the mind of the secretary to inform the police and risk a body of policemen more suited to control pickets during an industrial dispute when only half a dozen objectors are likely to show up but there appears to be no danger of crying 'wolf'. I have seen a Ford Transit full of police plus three motorcycle riders sent to control the grand total of three anti-fieldsports demonstrators but the police involved seemed rather to enjoy their day out. Although it would be stretching the story a little too far to say that one or two officers are now fully paid up members of the hunt, nevertheless they showed a great interest in the proceedings and the police bikes proved very useful in keeping up with hounds!

Good relations with the police are obviously important. If the hunt is fortunate enough to boast a local 'bobby', every effort should be made to include him in any social events, and the knowledge that the kennel's kettle is always on can encourage the police to take an interest in what is happening during the hunting season. The local policeman starts out with a great advantage for if and when he is called on by the hunt he is likely to know the area well.

When a patrol comes from further afield, social visits to the kennels could be used to show them on a map the extent of the country. Boundaries, footpaths, short cuts, lay-bys and green lanes can be pointed out and, in the event of help being needed, both parties will know the lie of the land and be able to act promptly.

One of the golden rules when encountering 'antis' must be to ignore them. They generally stick to the public highways anyway and on a good scenting day will probably not worry hounds; indeed some huntsmen to whom I have spoken claim that their beagles can hunt straight through a group of protesters. Under no circumstances should a situation be created where a confrontation between the hunt and the league occurs. It will almost inevitably be unpleasant, with abuse and fists flying in both directions. If the action ends ultimately in a court case, this is often the publicity for which the 'antis' are looking.

In the unfortunate event of objectors knowing the whereabouts

Antis, police and hunt followers. The car in the foreground belongs to the couple nearest to it, who feel strongly about hunting as a sport; they are content to make their presence felt without causing any obstruction. A police presence may be necessary but the regular followers here continue the enjoyment of their sport without fearing any unpleasantness *(Geoff Burch)*

of the kennels and meeting there, the police should be called before the hound van moves off. The hunt will, in all probability, be on a better wicket legally whilst still on private land rather than letting the antis follow it to the meet where the police cannot act due to the venue being a public place.

The legal situation

Each incident will be treated by the police on its individual merits. If for instance a meet is being held in Farmer Blogg's farmyard, obviously by his invitation, and anti-bloodsports demonstrators appear, then the farmer will probably wish to involve the police who will naturally turn out but cannot really remove the protesters unless violence or malicious damage ensues. When this does happen the whole situation changes from being a civil matter to one with criminal repercussions and then the police are quite within their rights to class the perpetrators as trespassers and remove them from the site, where necessary charging them with criminal offences which they have committed.

The whole subject of trespass seems to be very vague. No one can

181

be classed as a trespasser if he is merely standing in a field observing the wildlife. If, on the other hand, it seems that he is involved in causing some form of damage, then apparently it is permissible to remove him with as much force as is 'reasonable'. No longer are landowners or their employees allowed to threaten and force people from their land as they were fifty years ago. Nowadays, if the owner or his employee were eventually taken to court on a case of 'assault', it would be difficult to prove that the force used was justified.

It is not often realised that footpaths and bridleways are highways in the same way that roads are highways. Council authorities are responsible for keeping paths clear but the landowner is liable for keeping stiles or gates in good repair, a point worth knowing when encountering the 'anti' who appears to have the legal situation taped and begins to quote his rights whilst on a public footpath or bridle-way.

Again, it is useful to know that in these circumstances a person's right to use a highway is limited to passing and re-passing on bona fide business. The law states that it is permissible to sit and rest but to be involved in anything which is not 'referable to a right of passage' renders the person a trespasser. In the same way, a person who drives on any footpath or similar highway without lawful authority is liable to conviction. However, an offence is not committed when a vehicle is parked on a footpath provided that it is within 15 yards of the road. This is not a right but it is not an offence.

A person who parks his vehicle anywhere off the road is committing an offence against the owner of the soil.

There is a difficulty in enforcing the above rule, especially on the hunting day when cars belonging to hunt staff and followers are given permission by the landowner to park on his land. Then it would appear that no offence is committed. The drivers are, however, subject to the part of the Road Traffic Act which makes reckless and dangerous driving an offence — a technicality which could prove useful when a demonstrator may be thought to be putting the safety of hounds at risk.

There is a limit to what the user of a footpath can take with him. A stick or dog is described in the legal books as being a 'natural accompaniment' but would an aerosol can of Anti-mate, a sack soaked with aniseed, urine or some such in order to set up a false trail, or even a placard proclaiming the beaglers' inhumanity to wild animals, be classed as the same?

The above deals with just some of the problems of beagling today. Obviously individual packs will have their individual problems and may claim that I have not dealt with the fact that a neighbouring gamekeeper is intent on poisoning the hounds because they inadvertently ran through his best drive a day before his governor's friends were due to shoot, or that in the last house of the new estate built on the kennel's doorstep there is a person who seems to have nothing better to do than write to the local newspaper describing the activities of the sadists living next door. There are ways of overcoming such incidents, impossible though it may seem. An invitation to the kennels, showing hounds, explaining what happens during the hunting day and how difficult it is to stop twenty-five couple of hounds in full cry, may help. A whisky bottle accompanying the dissertation may also pay unforeseen dividends!

Looking beyond the eighties

What of the future? Estates will get smaller rather than larger, roads larger rather than smaller, and, as more and more people are forced into a town life, losing their country instincts in the process, opposition to fieldsports will inevitably become greater.

In conclusion

Fieldsports of whatever nature have traditionally followed the same lines. Whilst researching for greater detail and asking questions of experienced masters and huntsmen, I have found that what people say today and what sporting writers of the past have committed to print remain basically the same.

Of course veterinary procedures have progressed. The consultant of fifty years ago who diagnosed a disease as being that of 'hysteria' would today be treated with a wry smile from his modern counterpart, who knows that the all-embracing term cannot be treated by one dose of a 'wonder medicine' and a few hours spent by the hound in a darkened room.

The importance of hygiene was given adequate mention in the chapter concerning life in the kennels but if the measures outlined are not strictly adhered to there could be problems in the future.

Short of a revolution in the hunting world, there is little chance that feeding and exercise procedures will change but, again on the lookout for possible problems in the future, the views of scientists and veterinary surgeons should perhaps be mentioned here.

'Raw meat and grass runs are detrimental to the wellbeing of hounds': an outrageous statement and one which would have the hunters of yesteryear revolving, let alone turning, in their graves. Nevertheless, it seems that infection by parasites could be dramatically reduced by replacing grass paddocks with concrete runs. Transmission of internal parasites is facilitated by the aggregation of large numbers of hounds sharing grass exercise runs. Although the life cycles of certain types of helminths are not fully understood, it seems that a puppy can acquire infection from its dam soon after birth.

As to the question of feeding, the veterinary surgeon from whom I sought advice regarding the welfare of hounds in the kennels was horrified to be told that almost all packs feed raw meat and offal. In his opinion this type of diet, fed continually, can only lead to problems.

There are at least five species of the tapeworm genus which occur in the small intestines of canines, all of which are more likely to present themselves in an environment where only raw meat is fed. In a study carried out seven years ago, it was found that the presence of tapeworms differed greatly between two foxhound packs which were kennelled in the same locality but fed by two completely separate methods. One was fed on commercial dog food, supplemented with farm livestock casualties from its immediate farm environment; the other only on livestock carcasses from farms from further afield plus offal, sheep's heads and so on from the local abattoir. In this particular study those hounds fed on the proprietary types of food had only 13.3 per cent of tapeworms in their body whilst those fed entirely on offal and casualties contained 87.6 per cent — quite an appreciable difference and one which speaks for itself.

Although abattoir surveys have found worms present in almost all varieties of uncooked meat and that the heaviest areas of infection are in establishments where animals are fed on this type of diet, hounds may also pick up infection from carcasses found on the hunting day and so it behoves every master to impress on his staff the need for vigilance, especially in areas in which sheep are to be encountered.

Fortunately, many hunts are tended by forward-thinking people and although I have included the above in an effort to provoke thought and to point out the possibilities of things being done in a different way, some of these people are already prepared to experiment in order to find out what is best for their hounds.

One such pack, for instance, has found that young puppies walked at the kennels rather than with individual puppy walkers, and kennelled together, are more inclined to enter as a pack and not as individuals. Only a small step, it has to be admitted, but one made with the future well-being of beagling at heart.

Although beagling has never really been a male dominated sport, and a cross-section of its followers seem to split quite nicely into a fifty/fifty ratio, it is not often that the huntsman is a woman. Why this should be the case, I do not know, especially when one considers that in general women make better dog handlers than do men. There are, however, a handful of lady masters, many of whom contribute greatly to the hunt by combining other duties such as that of secretary as is the case with Mrs Jean Dunn of Hunsley Beacon, or kennel huntsman in the case of Miss Angus of the Mid Essex.

The Colne Valley beagles in 1969, with the author on the extreme right indulging his early love of beagling — once gained, never lost (by courtesy of the *Huddersfield Examiner*)

Female whippers-in abound but their numbers seem to be the same as they were when I first became interested in beagling some seventeen years ago so it does not appear to be valid to suggest that it was a lack of female whippers-in in the past which caused a lack of female huntmen and that this imbalance will now automatically be redressed.

It seems that many ladies who enjoy the sport of beagling are content to remain 'behind the scenes' and, without in any way wishing to reduce their capabilities, it is a good job that they are, for many a social event would be poorer without their organisation and competence at fund-raising, collecting raffle prizes, cooking and monetary prowess — all essential points if the hunt is to be financially successful.

Whilst on the subject of women and beagling, perhaps now is an ideal time to point out that although I have referred to hounds, hunt staff and followers throughout the book in the masculine, it has only been for the sake of convenience. For 'he', the readers should accept that 'she' would apply equally as well.

Finally, if anything I have written should induce even one or two who have no experience of the sport to try it, or to make the more experienced realise that there is always something to learn and a different, possibly easier, way to achieve the same end result, then I shall be delighted and they will not regret it, especially if there is in their make-up that wonderful passion which once a person catches he will never lose — the love of beagling.

GLOSSARY

All on Message from whipper-in to huntsman to tell him that hounds are all present and correct.

Babble When a hound speaks unnecessarily.

Benches Sleeping platforms in the kennels.

Best When a hare has given a good hunt and staff decide to leave her for another day, she is said to have been given 'best'.

Blank When no hares have been seen or hunted, a day is said to be 'blank'.

Blood Give young hounds their first kill.

Blowing away By use of the horn, the huntsman informs the followers that hounds are on the line of a hare.

Bone The size and strength of a hound is often referred to by his 'bone'.

Brace Two hares.

Break up The hounds are said to 'break up' the hare at the end of a successful hunt.

Bye-day A day's hunting which does not appear on the published list of appointments.

Cap, the Money collected, normally by the secretary, from casual followers who do not subscribe to the hunt.

Cast A huntsman casts his hounds when they have lost the scent and need his help to show them the way to go in order to re-commence the hunt.

Check Hounds check when they have momentarily lost the scent of the hare.

Chop When a hare is killed by the hounds before she has had a chance to run, she is said to have been 'chopped'.

Country The area hunted by a particular pack of hounds.

Couple Two hounds. A pack is known by couples and counted as couples, never individuals. One couple, two or more couples.

Couples, or Couplings Two collars joined by swivels, linking two hounds together, usually to attach a young hound to an older, more experienced hound when out on exercise.

Coursing Hunting by sight.

Cry Sound given from entire pack when hunting.

Draft The practice of sending a hound to another pack because it is not suitable for the pack which bred it.

Drawing Looking for a hare at the start of the hunt. Also used when choosing hounds for the hunting day.

Enter Starting a hound on its hunting career.

Feather Hounds are said to be 'feathering' when they take a sudden and more active interest during drawing, usually because they have come across a faint scent.

Field Followers of the hunt.

Flags At a hound show, hounds are shown on a small concrete square known as flags.

Foil The hare's scent is said to be foiled if it crosses other scents such as those of farm animals, artificial fertilisers and so on.

Glossary

Form Resting place for a hare.

Give tongue Noise made by hounds when hunting.

Head Turning the hare from its intended path — a heinous crime!

Heel If hounds pick up a scent and hunt the quarry towards where she has been rather than in the direction she is travelling, they are said to be hunting a 'heel' scent or trail.

Holding up For whatever reason, when the whips need to keep hounds to the huntsman in a tight group.

Holloa When the *hunted* (most important, this) hare has been seen by a follower, then he or she can 'holloa' to inform the huntsman of the hare's direction. It is then up to the huntsman to decide whether to lift the hounds to the holloa or let his pack work out the scent for themselves.

Hot bitch Used by the hunting fraternity to describe a bitch in season or on heat.

Lift Taking hounds to a holloa or view.

Line The scent of a hunted hare.

Mask Hare's head, sometimes mounted after a particularly good hunt.

Mute A hound which runs and hunts without giving tongue or speaking.

Own Pick up the scent.

Pad Hare's or hound's foot.

Point The actual distance from putting up the hare to the kill but taken as the crow flies.

Rate Correcting hounds for some misdemeanour, usually done by whips.

Riot When hounds hunt and chase anything other than the hare.

See-ho Rarely used, but means 'I have seen the hunted hare'. (Foxhunting equivalent is 'tally-ho'.)

Skirter Hound which cuts corners, not hunting the scent but anticipating the quarry's movements — not desirable behaviour.

Speak Hounds giving tongue.

Stale line An old scent.

Stern A hound's tail.

Tail hound One which is constantly left behind by the rest of the pack.

Trencher-fed Hounds kept by individual hunt members and then brought to the meet by their owners for the hunting day — more common in fell foxhunting packs than in any beagling packs.

View When followers see the quarry.

Walk Taking a young hound from the pack for 'private education' in the puppy walker's own home.

Walking out Hound exercise.

BIBLIOGRAPHY

Beaufort, The Duke of, *Fox Hunting* (David & Charles, 1980)

Brock, David, MFH, *To Hunt the Fox* (Seeley Services, 1937)

Burrows, Roger, *Wild Fox* (Pan Paperbacks, 1968)

Campbell, Ian, *A Practical Guide to the Laws of Footpaths and Bridleways* (Commons, Open Spaces and Footpaths Preservation Society, 1974)

Drabble, Phil, *What Price the Countryside?* (Michael Joseph, 1985)

Ewart Evans, George, and Thomson, David, *The Leaping Hare* (Faber and Faber, 1972)

Forbes, Commander W. B., RN, *Hounds, Gentlemen, Please!* (Hodder and Stoughton, 1911)

Fuller, Christopher, *An Urban Survey of Views on Wildlife Conservation* (1965)

Glover, H. (ed.), *A Standard Guide to Purebred Dogs* (Macmillan)

Hart, E., *Encyclopedia of Dog Breeds* (TFH Publications Inc)

Johnston, George, *The Basset Hound* (Saiga Publishing)

Johnston, George, *Hounds of France* (Saiga Publishing, 1979)

St Leger-Gordon, Douglas, *The Way of a Fox* (Scientific Book Club)

Shepherd, C. B., *Beagling* (Seeley Services, 1938)

Smith, Guy N., *Animals of the Countryside* (Saiga Publishing, 1980)

Tapper, Dr Stephan, *The Hare Project — A Final Report* (The Game Conservancy, 1983)

Thomas, Richard H., *The Politics of Hunting* (Gower Publishing Company Ltd, 1983)

Vandervell, Anthony, and Coles, Charles, *Game and the English Landscape* (Debrett, 1980)

Vesey-Fitzgerald, Brian, *It's My Delight* (Eyre and Spottiswoode, 1947)

Willoughby, The Hon Charles, *Come and Hunt* (Museum Press, 1952)

APPENDIX 1

The work and aims of the Association of Masters of Harriers and Beagles — Horn Park, Beaminster, Dorset DT8 3HB

The association was originally formed in 1891 by a group of hunting enthusiasts who wished to improve the standard of hound packs already in existence by maintaining stud books and allowing hounds entered in these books to compete against each other at the annual Peterborough hound show, which it also organised.

Since then the association's duties have become far more widespread and their rules and objectives provide a most effective and very necessary governing body to which any hare-hunting pack registered as a member can turn to for advice. In return, however, these members must maintain some high standards both morally and performance-wise and undertake to preserve good relations amongst the general public, many of whom see the hunting person as being nothing more than a sadistic barbarian.

When setting up a pack of hounds it is not merely a case of building kennels, appointing oneself as master and huntsman, and disappearing into the countryside looking for a hare to kill. For a start, unless one is a member of the association it will be extremely difficult to obtain any draft hounds with which to hunt, as surplus hounds suitable for drafting and stallion hounds from which to breed are normally offered only to existing members by fellow members, a policy which is made generally known to its members by the association.

Having overcome this first obstacle, it is advisable for any aspiring master of hounds to apply in writing for registration to the association and to make sure that the country over which he intends to hunt is not already being used by some other hare-hunting pack.

If accorded (which would be very doubtful since most of Britain is already registered, with the exception of parts of Cornwall, the highlands and mountains of Scotland and Wales and the highly populated industrial conurbations) the registration would operate for a probationary period of at least one season during the course of which the new pack would be expected to hunt fairly the country which it intends to claim, and well outside the boundaries of other, well-established packs. Should a favourable decision then be given, the newly appointed member has to be prepared to adhere to the rules of the association — which are set out in its annual handbook — and to pay any fees and subscriptions which may be called for by the joint committee of the association.

These rules not only include a code of conduct but also a set of rules which concerns the huntsman's behaviour on a hunting day, entries in the stud books and also rules with which the hunt must acquaint themselves before entering for Peterborough or any similar hound show. Briefly, all hounds must belong to a recognised pack of harriers or beagles which hunts a recognised country and must be registered in the stud book or, in the case of unentered hounds, have been bred by a registered hunt, be the progeny of stud-book hounds or a stud-book hound. Beagles must not exceed 16 inches in height, harriers not more than 21 inches. Further, more technical points and rules dealing with both showing and entries to the stud book are the concern of the masters of each pack and they can find this information in the current handbook.

An arrangement exists between the association and the Kennel Club whereby the latter has undertaken not to accept for registration, or allow to be shown under club rules, hounds coming from packs other than those registered by the association. In practice, however, no pack even attempts to register or show under Kennel Club rules, the standards required being so different, but the arrangement operates to underline the difference between those who breed for hunting and those who breed for showing and commercial purposes. It is felt by the association's committee '. . . that this arrangement is absolutely necessary if the association is to function effectively as the governing body of hare hunting and at the same time to foster the breeding of hounds for this purpose'. With a view to maintaining and improving the quality of the blood registered in the association's stud book, this same committee stresses to all practising masters the importance of breeding only from hounds which have proved themselves to be absolutely sound in their hunting capabilities.

The association is not, however, content merely to sit in its ivory tower dispensing judgement and enforcing codes of conduct and, by means of national conferences and instruction, it assists in the training of both potential and serving hunt staffs with regard to breeding and kennel management. In an effort not only to help individual members but also to preserve the good name of the sport by providing an active liaison with many outside organisations, there is an advisory service which supplies literature covering subjects as diverse as how to deal with hunt saboteurs, information for the hunt secretary on VAT, contracts of employment and pension schemes. The association also carefully monitors acts of parliament, both proposed and enforced, when it feels that such litigation and activities may affect beagling at either a national or local level.

Because of the many obvious benefits, only a few of which are outlined here, the association's numerous members are only too pleased to abide by the rules, secure in the knowledge that they are made for the future well-being of the sport. In the rare case of either master or hunt falling foul of these rules, there is a set way of dealing with the suspected 'offender': after the committee has heard all sides of the dispute, during which the master or hunt in question is given ample opportunity to provide a fully documented statement and to make a personal appeal, the association has the power to terminate membership and remove the hunt from the list of recognised packs. In such an event the hounds owned by that pack immediately become ineligible for entry in any future stud book.

Any dispute arising from hunting can also be brought to the attention of the association by a hunt: if the person or persons which are affected by the problem agree to his doing so, then it is possible for the master to bring the case before the committee on the proviso that the hunt submits to the eventual decision made by the association.

APPENDIX 2
Beagle packs officially recognised by the
Association of Masters of Harriers and Beagles

Obviously masterships and hunt premises change from time to time. Although there may be more than one master, it is the intention only to include the name of the pack and the first-named master who appears in the list drawn up annually by the association. Remember, too, that the master may live out of the country over which a particular pack hunts and therefore the address is not necessarily indicative of the hunt's boundaries.

Airedale
J.W.D. Paisley, West Moor House Farm, Middleton, Ilkley, Yorks LS29 0DW (Ilkley 609245)
Aldershot
D.R. Clinkard, The Kennels, Oxney Farm, Bordon, Hants GU35 9LH (Bordon 2262)
Ampleforth
M.G.O. Bridgeman, Ampleforth College, York YO6 4EW (Ampleforth 426)
Beacon
M.D. Milburn, Bywood, Dunkeswell, Honiton, Devon (Luppitt 658)
Black Combe and District
S. Ellwood, High Moorside Farm, Holmrook, Cumbria CA19 1YD (Holmrook 234)
Blean
Mrs J.B. McKeever, Waterham Farm, Hernhill, Faversham, Kent (Faversham 751 227)
Bleasdale
D.A.H. Grayling, Lyvennet, Crosby Ravensworth, Penrith CA10 3JP (Ravensworth 282)
Bolebroke
R.I.M. Standring, Dacre Cottage, Withyham, East Sussex TN11 4BE (Hartfield 388)
Brighton and Storrington Foot
J.R. Watters, Pensfold Farm, Bucks Green, Horsham, West Sussex RH12 3BU (Rudgwick 2408)
Britannia
Admiral Sir James Eberle KCB, Village Farm, Holne, Newton Abbot, S. Devon (Poundsgate 281)
Catterick
Major W.H.D.N. Robotham, The Old Vicarage, Marygate, Barton, Darlington DL10 6LD (Barton 772)
Cheshire
Dr M. Parkes, Newfield Hall, Minshull Vernon, Middlewich, Cheshire CW10 0LR (Church Minshull 667)

Chilmark
G.H. Harland, 4 Chalice Hill Close, Glastonbury, Somerset BA6 8AY (Glastonbury 31509)
Christchurch and Farley Hill
A.R. Fitzalen Howard, The Grove, Shotover Park, Wheatley, Oxford
Claro
Brig A.A. Seaton CBE, Warren House, Thorpefield, Thirsk, North Yorks (Thirsk 24426)
Clifton Foot
K.S. Gardner, 81 West Town Road, Backwell, Bristol (Flax Bourton 2144)
Colchester Garrison
Col D.F. Easten MC, Bowdens Cottage, Wormingford, Colchester, Essex CO6 3BA (Bures 227246)
Colne Valley
P.J. Hole, Laver Head, Green Lane, Shibden, Halifax, West Yorks HX3 7TB (Halifax 206624)
Colston
T. Challands, Colston Farm, Billingborough Fen, Sleaford, Lincs
Constantine
A.V. Alway, Silverhill Farm, Treculliacks, Constantine, Cornwall
Crowcombe
J.J. Price, Oakgreen Houses, Oake, Taunton, Somerset TA4 1AS (Bradford-on-Tone 469)
De Burgh and North Essex Harehounds
J.S. Humphrey, Coldharbour Farm, Tilty, Dunmow, Essex (Great Easton 257)
Derbyshire, Nottinghamshire and Staffordshire
G. De Ville, Victory Farm, Doveridge, Derby (Uttoxeter 2450)
Derwent Valley
C.M. Tetley, Manor Farm, Little Habton, Malton, North Yorks YO18 0UA (Malton 638)
Dummer
G. A. Craghill, Field Barn, Coates, Cirencester, Glos (Cirencester 66059)
Ecclesfield
The Earl of Wharncliffe, Wharncliffe House, Wortley, Sheffield (Wortley 882331)
Emlyn
T.M.R. Holland, Big House Farm, Pendine, Carms (Pendine 256)
Eton College
H.J. Gray-Cheape, Manor House, Eton, Windsor
Forest and District
R.F. May, Long Ridge, Sutton, Macclesfield, Cheshire (Macclesfield 2250)
Glyn Celyn
Lt Col A.S. Jervis, Verlands, Erwood, Builth Wells, Powys (Builth Wells 248)
Holcombe Rogus
R.G. Adams, Burnell's Coombe, Blackdown Cross, Crediton, Devon EX17 3QQ (Cheriton Bishop 463)

Holme Valley
C. Ford, 18 Grasscroft Avenue, Honley, Huddersfield, West Yorks (Huddersfield 662976)
Hunsley Beacon
Mrs J.M. Dunn, The Old Rectory, Harswell, York YO4 4LE (Harswell 60226)
Hurcott
G.J. Sprosen, 2 Batham Road, Kidderminster, Worcs (Kidderminster 68304)
Hydfer Hounds
Dr D.G. Rees, Traianglas Vicarage, Trecastle, Brecon, Powys (Powys 427)
Ilminster
N.J. Miers-Raby, Brook Farm, North Curry, Taunton, Somerset (Taunton 490976)
Isle of Wight Foot
Lt Col P.S. Mitcheson DSO OBE, 12 Yelfs Road, Ryde, IOW (Ryde 64800)
Marhamchurch Foot
A.J. Rickard, Haye House, Callington, Cornwall (Callington 2270)
Marlborough College
The College, Marlborough, Wiltshire
Meon Valley
Miss J. Wilkinson, Dundridge Farm, Bishops Waltham, Hants (Bishops Waltham 2608)
Mid Essex
Miss P. Angus, Black Log, Clavering, Saffron Walden, Essex CN11 4RR (985 279)
Monmouthshire
A.J. Womack, Pencoed-Cae, Pant-Yr-Esk, Newbridge, Gwent (0495 243798)
Newcastle and District
Col R.M. Gibson, Simonburn Cottage, Humshaugh, Hexham, Northumberland (0434 81 402)
New Forest
J.H. Clark, Meadow Farm, Sway Road, Tiptoe, Lymington, Hants (Lymington 682432)
Norfolk
J.S. Austen, Low Farm, Caston Road, Carbrooke, Thetford, Norfolk (095 383 262)
North Bucks
W.R. George, South Brook Cottage, Wilden, Bedford MK44 2PE (0234 771157)
North Dartmoor
T.J. Whitley, Hedge Barton, Widecombe-in-the-Moor, Newton Abbot, Devon (Manaton 219)
North Staffordshire Moorland
D. Mosedale, Hunter's Lodge, Old Lane, Brown Edge, Stoke-on-Trent ST6 8TG (0782 503328)

North Warwickshire
J. Sutton, 29 Little Warton Road, Warton, Tamworth, Staffordshire (0827 893414)
Oakley Foot
A.J. Bolesworth, Redhill Barn Cottage, Burton Bandalls, Loughborough, Leics LE12 5TE (Loughborough 214924)
Old Berkeley
J.F. Robinson, Marston Fields Farm, North Marston, Buckinghamshire MK18 3PG (029667 215)
Palmer Milburn
R.J.H.D. Palmer, Butlers Farm, Beenham, Reading (0734 713330)
The Park
Lt Cdr W.F.P. Crutchley RN, Brown's Farm, Powerstock, Bridport, Dorset (030885 279)
Per Ardua
M. Salmon, Melwood Grange, Epworth, Doncaster, S. Yorks DN9 1AA (Epworth 87227)
Pevensey Marsh
Miss F. Harrison, 55 The Drive, Ersham Park, Hailsham, Sussex BH24 8HW (0323 840331)
Pimpernel
R.G.C. Clarke, Petersfinger Farm, Salisbury, Wilts (Salisbury 333645)
Pipewell Foot
D. Reynolds, Burdyke, Weekley, Kettering, Northamptonshire NN16 9UX (0536 82372)
Purbeck and Bovington
B.A. McSwiney, 6 The Orchard, Winfrith Newburgh, Dorchester, Dorset (Wardell 853331)
Radley College
A. Onslow, Radley College, Radley, Abingdon, Oxford (0235 25592)
Redhill
M.S.C. Heathcote, Lords Park Farm, St Neot, Liskeard, Cornwall (0579 20759)
RAC
P.G. Mayo, 4 Cottage, Swillbrook Farm, Minety, Malmesbury, Wilts
Royal Rock
R.B. Symonds, 2 Springfield, Hawarden, Deeside, Clwyd CH5 3DW (0244 536171)
Sandhurst
The Royal Military Academy, Sandhurst, Camberley, Surey (0276 63344 — Enquiries)
Shrivenham
R. R. Paling, Orchard House, Shrivenham, Swindon, Wilts SN6 8AW (Swindon 782214)
Shropshire
Col D.H. Tildesley, Tettenhall Court, Tettenhall, Wolverhampton (0902 751481)

South Herts
J.D. Ashby, Ivinghoe Aston Farm, Leighton Buzzard, Bedfordshire LU7 9DG (0525 221678)
Sproughton Foot
Miss P.M. Paul, Woodside, Constitution Hill, Ipswich, Suffolk IP1 3RH (Ipswich 52055)
Stoke Hill
A.J. Bennett, Linhayes, Perkins Village, Farringdon, Exeter, Devon (Woodbury 32428)
Stokesley Farmers
H.B. Wrightson, White House, Hutton Rudby, Yarm, N. Yorkshire (Hutton Rudby 700397)
Stowe
Stowe School, Buckingham
Stowford Hunt Club
P. Mayne, 17 North Road, Lifton, Devon PL16 0DS
Surrey and North Sussex
D.J. Dickens, Moor Lodge, Park Lane, Reigate, Surrey RH2 8JX (Reigate 43295)
Taw Vale
G. R. Cox, Cannington, Witheridge, Tiverton, Devon (Tiverton 860524)
Tees Valley
G.R.H. Allan, Kilmaha, 26 Low Green, Gainford, Darlington DL2 3DS (Darlington 730357)
Trinity Foot
The Kennels, Cambridge Road, Barton, Cambridgeshire (Comberton 2362)
Valley
D.W. Jones, 30 Park Crescent, Bargoe, Mid Glam CF8 8PN (0443 838286)
Warwickshire
P.I.R. Comber, Churchill Cottage, Bishopton Hill, Stratford-upon-Avon, Warwickshire (0789 297381)
Weardale
S.W. Beckett, Holywell Hall, Brancepeth, Durham (0385 780369)
Wentlog
G. Best, Beagledale, Penylan, Bassaleg, Newport, Gwent (Castleton 680565)
West Down
E.P. Hookway, Hazelhurst, Langleigh Road, Ilfracombe, Devon (Ilfracombe 62980)
Wick and District
A.J.A. Seymour Williams, The Old Rectory, Syston, Mangotsfield, Bristol BS17 3LR (027 582 2434)
Wiltshire and Infantry
Lt Col J.S. McLaren OBE, Chancel End House, Heytesbury, Warminster, Wilts BA12 0EE (0985 40321)
Wye College
I.R. Hurst, 76 Upper Bridge Street, Wye, Ashford, Kent

Wyre Forest
R.J. Colver, Woodside Cottage, Raycombe Lane, Codington, Ledbury, Herefordshire (Ledbury 3985)

Harrier packs also registered with the association

Aldenham	North Norfolk
Axe Vale	Pendle Forest and Craven
Bolventor	Rockwood
Cambridgeshire	Ross
Cotley	Rufford Forest
Dart Vale and Haldon	South Pool
Dunston	Staffordshire Moorland
Easton	Taunton Vale
Eryri	Vale of Lune
High Peak	Waveney
Holcombe	Wensleydale
Minehead	Weston and Banwell
Modbury	Windermere

APPENDIX 3
Harehounds registered with the
Masters of Basset Hounds Association

Secretary
R. Hudson, Yew Tree Cottage, Haselton, Cheltenham, Gloucestershire

Albany
Crealy
De Burgh and North Essex Harehounds
East Lincs Harehounds
Hickworthy
Leadon Vale
South Wales
Westerby
West Lodge Harehounds
West Oxfordshire

ACKNOWLEDGEMENTS

The author would like to thank the following: Lyn and Roy Clinkard and the Aldershot Beagles — the time spent in their company, the information volunteered and the facilities for photography are much appreciated; Col M. St G. Pallot, ex-Master of the Sandhurst, and their huntsman Michael Jackson; John Kirkpatrick, Secretary to the Association of Masters of Harriers and Beagles; Dr Stephen Tapper of the Game Conservancy; Mr Bradley Viner, The British Small Animals Veterinary Association; Laurence Pollinger Ltd, for permission to use information and material from *It's My Delight* by Brian Vesey-Fitzgerald; Richard Hedger and Geoff Burch for the excellent photographs and Gina Arnold (for the ones they didn't manage!); Miss J. Wilkinson and Mr C. Vivian and the Meon Valley Beagles; Mr Patrick Comber, Warwickshire Beagles; Lt Col G. Thompson, Wensleydale Harriers; Dr D.G. Rees, Hydfer Harehounds; Mrs O.M. Weston, East Lincs Harehounds; Paul Jelly BA; William Watt; George Johnston.

INDEX